CHESHIRE

Edited by Michelle Warrington

P186

First published in Great Britain in 1998 by
POETRY NOW YOUNG WRITERS
1-2 Wainman Road, Woodston,
Peterborough, PE2 7BU
Telephone (01733) 230748

HB ISBN 0 75430 263 6
SB ISBN 0 75430 264 4

FOREWORD

With over 63,000 entries for this year's Cosmic competition, it has proved to be our most demanding editing year to date.

We were, however, helped immensely by the fantastic standard of entries we received, and, on behalf of the Young Writers team, thank you.

The Cosmic series is a tremendous reflection on the writing abilities of 8-11 year old children, and the teachers who have encouraged them must take a great deal of credit.

We hope that you enjoy reading *Cosmic Cheshire* and that you are impressed with the variety of poems and style with which they are written, giving an insight into the minds of young children and what they think about the world today.

CONTENTS

Meredydd Jones	62
Mark Watson	63
Kate Gibson	64
Ella Dore	65
Fern McDonald	66
Helen Monaghan	67
Natalie Dent	68
Wendy Baranowska	68
Jenny Jones	69
Sarah Everton	70
Charlotte Royle	71
David Gray	72

Firs Primary School

Daniel Sweeney	72
Louise Pennington	73
Lee Hulse	73
Lee Bolland	74
Christopher Bird	74
Garry Hebb	75
Adam Robson	75
Chandelle Henry	76
Natalie Bailey	76
Sarah Jones	76
Katrina Sweetser-Hawkes	77
Sarah Willis	78

Greenbank School

Juan C Herraiz	78
Sophie Whittle	79
Matthew Williamson	79
Jenna Wayne	80
Rachel Sheldon	80
Richard Rawlings	81
Tim Watkins	82
Matthew Griffin	82
Sophia Copley	83

Richard Hodgins	83
Felicity Rankin	84
Mark Bowen	84
Adrian Wu	85
Sophie Bryan	85
Emma Dickinson	86
Peter Crocker	86
Andrew Dickson	87
Andrew McGeorge	88
Matthew Galloway	88
Nicola Bowen	89
Marcus Budgett	89
Andrew Jakubowski	90
Carla Rankin	90

Hurstclough Primary School

Rebecca Berry	91
Kirsty Jordan	91

Park Road Primary School

Ann-Marie Lawrence	92
Laura Howe	92
Stephanie Hamer	93
Andrew Colclough	93
Hayley Fallon	94
Justine Woolley	94
Nadine Martynuik	95
Carolyn Fletcher	96
Ryan Parker	96
Charlotte Yeoman	97
Alex Jones	97
Rachel Cahill	98
Lynsey Wright	98

Prospect Vale Primary School

Nicola Camm	99
Rebecca Winder	99

Faye Daniels	100
Katie Doughty	100
Laura Dorsett	101
Shuhaib Shaffi	101
Sarah Marchant	102

Ridge Hill Primary School

Anthony Dando	102
Claire Walton	103
Samantha Lee	103
Sophie Booth	104
Richard Flanagan	104
Olivia Burgess	105
Tanya Murphy	105
Emma Hogg	106
Sarah Chatterton	106
Daniel Forrester	107
Jaya Patel	107
Gareth Culpin	108
Daryl Cornthwaite	108
Christopher Alexander	109
Stacey Healey	109
Leanne Waddock	110
Kayleigh Morris	110
Rachel Heap	111

St Basil's RC Primary School, Widnes

Ashley Parker	111
Katie Hodgson	112
Samantha Pye	112
Alan Hyland	113
Robert Rolt	113
Samantha Knight	114
Laura Pitt	114
Debbie Carmon	115
Asheligh Pierce	115
Elizabeth Allen	116
Hannah Edwards	117

Scott Jameson	192
Kyle Burns	192
Joe Woods	193
Derek Wiswall	193
Yvonne Byrom	194
Mark Hamilton	195
Katie Silcock	196
Ashia Thompson	196
David Lawton	197
Scott Oliver	198
Phillip Bartsch	199
Kyle Jerram	199
Sarah Holbrook	200
Andrew Reilly	201
Sarah Davies	202
Andrew Jack	202
Louise Illidge	203
Kerry Purvis	203
Steven Burnett	204
Ashley Wright	204
John Dutton	205
Faye Schön	206
Francesca Wright	206
Kerry-Anne McIntosh	207
Jaclyn Thomas	207
Mark Crowley	208
Wendy Osborne	208

Willaston CP School

Rebecca Taylor	209
Charlotte Wilson	209
Samantha Taylor	210
Lee Towers	211
Kathryn Alcock	211
Natasha Jackson	212
Aryan Sadler	212
Jonathan Colenso	213

THE POEMS

CHRISTMAS

All I hear on Christmas morning
is my brothers and my parents yawning.
We all go rambling down the stairs
to see all the presents on the chairs.
All we can hear is ripping and tearing
as we rip off the paper which the presents are wearing.
I can smell the Christmas turkey cooking,
of which my mum is always looking.
I go to church then come back home,
thank you for listening to my Christmas poem.

Ryan Donnelly (10)

SPY

I spy with my little eye
Something flying in
the sky.
Why?
Why?
Did I spy something
Flying in the sky?
It was a little
Fly.

Hi! Said the little fly,
Flying by in the sky.
The fly said
'Bye'
As it flew
by.

Lewis Walters (10)
Bankside School

MICKEY AND MILLY

Mickey and Milly were always
moaning and groaning
when I'm telephoning.

And when I have finished
telephoning,
Mickey and Milly
stop moaning and groaning!

Craig Vernon (10)
Bankside School

SPLASH POEM

Red hot burning fire from hell,
scorching, swirling so hot, shrivel
up and fall into a long, long sleep.

Icebergs floating in the blue sea,
beautiful and calm shining in the sun.

The yellow sun shining down on
the world, happy and bright, smiling
with earth's delight.

Coloured swirls turning, turning around
till *whoosh* it stops.

Diamonds glistening in a cave protected
by a fearsome dragon breathing fire.

Diamond people eating diamond cakes
dancing to diamond music.

Heather Dolan (10)
Barnton Junior School

SOUNDS OF THE FOREST

Howling, whistling wind
Crackling, crunching leaves
Squeaking, rustling mice
Screeching, beeping cars
Howling, barking foxes
Tweeting, chirping birds
Talking, shouting people.

Sarah Christie (8)
Barnton Junior School

THE LEAF

Yellow like the sun
Orange like the sunset
Pointed and smooth
Twisting and turning
Blowing in the cold air
Like a paper plane.

Roxanne Todd (9)
Barnton Junior School

THE FOREST

Snapping	falling	tree
Barking	happy	dogs
Clip	clapping	horses
Rushing	bubbling	streams
Digging	scrapping	badgers
Bouncing	hoping	rabbits.

Darren Malam (8)
Barnton Junior School

I Am Happy When I

Play with my hamster
Go to my nan's
Write a letter
Go on a school trip
Draw a picture
Do mental arithmetic
Plant seeds
Make a Viking boat
Have a birthday
Play outside
Go to Alton Towers
Wake up on Christmas Day.

Timothy Clarke (9)
Barnton Junior School

The Amazing House

The walls are made of purple mud.
The chimney is like a roller-coaster.
The roof is made of black crocodiles.
On top of the roof sits a blue tiger.
The windows are made of water
and they let in pink sun.
The door is covered in yellow birds' feathers.
Gloves grow on the orange tree.
Crimson pizza bushes line the path.
The leaves in my garden look like grey counters.
A lizard lives in my amazing house.

Christopher Myatt (8)
Barnton Junior School

THE LEAF

A brown leaf
Like an eye,
Hanging from a tree,
A gale came,
The leaf floated for a while,
It twirled and twisted,
It rocked, turned and landed,
Like a plane crashing.
It looked like it had changed
Into a feather.
And back to a leaf again.
But it didn't.

Sam Atherton (9)
Barnton Junior School

SOUNDS OF THE FOREST

Cracking, snapping twigs
Stiff, groaning roots
Running, splashing streams
Scratching, scraping foxes
Sniffing, snuffling badgers
Tapping, banging woodpeckers
Hooting, screeching owls
Puffing, panting cyclists
Laughing, chattering children.

James Sissons (8)
Barnton Junior School

THE AMAZING HOUSE

The walls of my house are made out of brown plates.
The chimney is like a green bird.
The roof is made of blue clay.
The windows are made of purple cheese
And they let in black sun.
The door is covered with grey sunflowers.
Mars bar trees grow in the garden.
Pink rock bushes edge the path.
The leaves look like orange fish.
An invisible cat lives in my
Amazing house.

Christopher Rathbone (8)
Barnton Junior School

THE AMAZING HOUSE

The walls of my house are invisible.
The chimney is like a yoghurt pot with a spoon in it.
The roof is made of slimy tadpoles.
On top of the roof sits a gigantic monster.
The windows are made of delicious birthday cake
and they let in red sunlight.
The door is covered in red and black fungi.
Pepsi Max trees grow in the garden.
Home-made lasagne bushes edge the path.
The leaves look like red and white crystals.
A business of ferrets live in my amazing house.

Samantha Rutter (8)
Barnton Junior School

THE AMAZING HOUSE

The walls of my house are made of green crisps
The chimney is like a bun
The roof is made of red jelly
On top of the roof sits a fairy cake
The windows are made of red glass
And they let in pink snow
The door is covered with black daisies
Ice lolly trees grow in the garden
Black soup bushes edge the path
The leaves look like pink fish scales
A Mr and Mrs Amazing live in my amazing house.

Katie Tatler (8)
Barnton Junior School

THE AMAZING HOUSE

The walls of my house are made of jelly.
The chimney is like a purple giraffe.
The roof is made of blue chocolate.
On top of the roof sits a black stegosaurus.
The windows are made of brown pulleys
and they let in green wind.
The door is covered with orange paper.
Money trees grow in the garden.
Yellow pick-a-mix sweet bushes edge the path.
The leaves look like golden books.
A silver parrot lives in my amazing house.

Shaun Ollier (7)
Barnton Junior School

COLOURS

Yellow is the colour of the sun shining in
the bright sky in the day.
Purple is the colour of the sky as the sun
sets at the end of the day.
Black is the colour of darkness at night
when the sun has disappeared.
Triangles are the shapes of expensive diamonds
that are worn by rich people.

Kirsty Griffiths (10)
Barnton Junior School

SOUNDS OF THE FOREST

Zooming, swishing wine
Clicking, clocking horses
Howling, hooting owls
Rumbling, rattling trains
Scratching, squeaking mice
Tapping, drilling woodpeckers.

Tom Goadby (8)
Barnton Junior School

SPLASH POEM

Brown is the colour of chocolate melting in your mouth,
Blue is the colour of a dolphin swimming in the blue sea,
Yellow is the colour of the warm, burning sun,
Orange is the colour of the wonderful sunset when it goes down,
A circle is the shape of a ring with a blue stone in it,
The oval is a shape of my sandy rabbit.

Rebecca Catterall (10)
Barnton Junior School

CLOUDS

I think clouds are great
They look like eggs on a plate
Sheep sleep on the hill
Clouds will give you a chill

I think clouds are great
People stop and wait
To look at them
I like clouds

Clouds on a rainy day
People stop and pray
But I say come again on
the next day.

Anthony Lacey (9)
Barnton Junior School

SPLASH POEM

The sky is glorious and blue,
The lovely, crisp sun on a warm summer's day,
The purple sky on a cold winter's night,
The brown soil dripping through your fingertips,
The nice circular sun on uncloudy day,
The fin of a dolphin in the nice light blue sea,
Peach is the lovely colour of a juicy peach when
you bite into it.

Helen Wood (9)
Barnton Junior School

MONSTERS, MONSTERS

Monsters, monsters everywhere,
Houses, castles, small ones in your hair.
Are they stone by day, monster by night?
Or do they just run when they see you in their sight.
Hallways, dungeons, under the stairs,
Big ones, small ones, hairy, hideous, huffy and scared.
What are they like? What do they eat?
Do they eat meat? I love monsters.
I've got one for a brother.
My mother loves him dearly, oh yes!
He is a little terror! He comes in my room,
Messes with my stuff, he never brushes his hair.
Even if you look at him, you'll be scared.
Monsters, monsters everywhere,
In the cupboard, under the stairs.
3 noses, 10 noses, what do they care?
Devouring people, antelope, hare.
Some are shy, some bold,
But they are all scary, I've been told.
So stay away from the monster pit,
Or you'll be very badly bit.

Jonathan Hayes (11)
Barnton Junior School

PLANTS AND TREES

Plants and trees
Lovely smell
And full of pollen too
No one picks them
Trees are full of birds that sing
Sun shines on the plants and trees.

Emma Hart (10)
Barnton Junior School

UNTITLED

A fire breathing dragon roaring
out its fiery red, flaming breath.
The straight lines of planes in the
light blue sky with the gush of
yellow from the sun.
On a cold night warmth from
the red fire.
Diamonds repeating the primary
colours red, yellow, blue.
As cool as the blue ice on a
frozen lake.
As red as a heart beating after
a long run.

Matthew Flanagan (10)
Barnton Junior School

THINKING OF OTHERS

Thinking of others in a great thing to do,
People of Bosnia,
People like you,
People in houses,
People on the streets,
People with no beds and seats,
People with no food to eat,
People with resting feet.
If you've really not got a clue,
Thinking of others is a great thing to do.

Jenny Davies (11)
Barnton Junior School

RICH

I'm going to my villa
And then to my yacht,
I'll sail to Hawaii
Where the sun's red hot.

I'll ride in my car
But which shall I take?
I'll take the Lamborghini
For a ride round the lake.

I'll go back to Spain
To visit my brother,
Then off to Manhattan
To visit my mother.

I'll fly from Manhattan
Over to France
To visit Nureyev
And learn how to dance.

I'll fly to Australia
And visit down under,
I'll go in my Porsche
And stop till Sunday.

I'll travel the world
Without ever a hitch,
I'll drive my Ferrari
Because I'm rich.

Adam Cornes (11)
Barnton Junior School

I SPY

I spy with my little eye,
A pink hedgehog in the sky.
I started to cry, I'll tell you why,
A sharp, spike fell right in my thigh.

Hannah Robinson (7)
Barnton Junior School

GUITAR HEAD

Guitar head is very strict
And he's got very, very long nails
His eyes are very bloodshot
And his nose is very big
He has six toes and very few fingers
His vampire teeth are very rammy
And there's blood dripping down from everywhere
So if you ever see him
Then do be very scared
Because he might just come and
Bite your head off!

Linzi Bell (11)
Barnton Junior School

CLOCKS

Red, yellow, green and blue,
the colours of my clocks.
Red, blue and green are primary colours.
Red is my square clock like a devil.
Blue is my funny shaped clock,
it is as if it is really cold.
Green is my favourite colour,
because it is bright and colourful.
Green and blue are dark colours
and red is hot, hot, hottt.

Samantha Jones (9)
Barnton Junior School

THE AMAZING HOUSE

The walls of my house are purple grass.
The chimney is like a blue bear.
The roof is made of yellow snake skin.
On top of the roof sits an orange lion.
The windows are made of brown cheese
And they let in crimson snow.
The door is covered with grey heather.
Ice-cream trees grow in the garden.
Purple galaxy bushes edge the path.
The leaves look like goldfish scales.
An alien lives in my amazing house.

Kenneth Dyson (8)
Barnton Junior School

UNTITLED

The light blue is the colour of the beautiful sky.
Red is the colour of the sun shining outside.
I think black is the colour of death.

Circle flowers in the glorious, glamorous shining red.
Hot sun, orange is the colour of the nice sunset
outside my house and my friend's house.

Jessica Woods (10)
Barnton Junior School

SNOZZCUMBER

He has two eyes and likes to spy
He has 7 legs and likes to beg
He's got a big belly which shakes like a jelly
He's got 4 arms, 4 tentacles too
He likes his bed so goodnight to you.

Zoe Shannon (10)
Barnton Junior School

UNTITLED

Red is like lava, molten rock flowing down the volcano.
Red makes me think of the devil, of evil spirits making mischief.
Red is a prime colour.
Red makes me feel warm, it is like a protecting colour.

Zak McCombie (9)
Barnton Junior School

I SPY

I spy with my little eye,
A yellow dog in the sky,
I always wondered if pigs could fly,
But a yellow dog - my oh my!

Nathan Thomson (8)
Barnton Junior School

UNTITLED

Black as the darkest night,
when ghosts come out after
a fatal crash.
As the watch goes tick, tock,
tick, tock at five past two.
Scars all over the body as the
ghost went up.
Bloodshot eyes watching,
watching, watching,
you.

Daniel Butterworth (9)
Barnton Junior School

THE JUNGLE

Trees swaying in the wind,
Cold rough rapids flowing down the river,
Birds squawking in the trees,
Non survivors lying dead,
The sound of aching trees in the wind,
Strange letters spread all over the jungle,
Lethal animals watching behind bushes,
Dusty sand in the wind,
Familiar footprints in the sand,
The green jungle.

James Salsbury (10)
Barnton Junior School

MISTY SHADOWS

Reptiles' scaly skin, sharp teeth, no care for babies.
Squares, four sides, pointed edges, sharp shapes.
Paint red, yellow, pink and blue paint.
Orange is the sunset shining down on us.
Purple, a warm colour, dark colour, a colour.
Night is a dark time, misty with shadows lurking round the corner.
Mammals are caring animals that care for its young.

Tiffany Beattie (10)
Barnton Junior School

SOUNDS OF THE FOREST

Slurping, slushy mud
Knocking, drilling woodpeckers
Stepping, gossiping people
Rushing, whirling stream
Sucking, twisting roots
Cracking, snapping branches
Creeping, sniffing badgers
Howling, digging foxes.

Andrew Booth (8)
Barnton Junior School

VIOLENT POOL

Bang! An explosion of someone
diving in,
Water splashing, pouncing on
the ropes,
Bubbles rise from the deep
place below,
A violent sea tossing and
turning,
White waves punch and push
the worn sides,
A wicked stormy pool crashing,
smashing, bashing,
Water sprays jumping up into
still air,
Suddenly a still, motionless,
serene, silence,
The sea has settled, it is calm,
quiet,
The rough sea has gone to sleep.

Lisa Cowap (10)
Beechwood CP School

THE IRON MAN

The glistening round eye.
Glaring and rolling.
Like a tiger ready to pounce on its prey.
To find the hand.

The stiff and silver hand.
Scuttling and creaking.
Like a lonely crab searching for a mate.
To find the arm.

Wriggling and struggling.
Like a fox in a trap.
To find a leg.

Hopping and jumping.
Like a headless chicken.
To find the head.

The head thoughtful but helpless.
Thinking and fidgeting.
Like a no-legged cheetah.

Robert Pownall (11)
Beechwood CP School

THE MERMAID

Before the free and turquoise sea
Beyond the rolling hills
There sits a mermaid, Emily
Staring down to the waters still.

Her features were expressionless
A daughter of the waves
Like a rock she sat, unmoving
Above the ebony caves.

The water never touched her tail
But still, she glistened wet
And a sight upon her lovely face
Was impossible to forget.

A lavish display of tiny pearls
Dressed the golden hair on her head
But never did a smile appear
On the lips so ruby red.

Her sparkling scales were silver
The shells on her body were bronze
False stories of this mermaid told
In sagas and in songs.

Finally, her sitting done
She slipped away from the shining sun
Into the ocean that called her away
There she remained, for how long I can't say.

Naomi Potter (10)
Beechwood CP School

IT SCARED ME!

I was walking home from my
friend's when I saw a shadow.
A place without light.
It was scary, spiky, weird and tall.
A place without a light.
It looked like a big, tall, hairy monster.
A place without light.
It looked like a picture from
one of my scary books.
A place without light.
I was scared, very scared indeed.
A place without light.
It was only a shadow.

Andrew West (8)
Bexton County Primary School

MY LITTLE SHADOW

I was lying in my bed when I saw a shadow
on my bedroom wall like a monster.
Shadows are formed when there's no light.
It was massive, fat and had jagged edges
and it looked very fierce.
Shadows are formed when there's no light.
It looked like a winter tree with pointy edges.
Shadows are formed when there's no light.
It was lurking in the kitchen.
Shadows are formed when there's no light.
It's only a shadow.

Jessica Cottingham (8)
Bexton County Primary School

A SHADOW

I was in the park and I saw
my shadow on the floor
A shadow is a black thing
It was a very dull shadow
A shadow is a black thing
It looked like a big giant
A shadow is a black thing
It was from my door
A shadow is a black thing
The shadow is an outline
A shadow is a black thing
The shadow is tall
A shadow is a black thing
It's very long
A shadow is a black thing
It's only a shadow!

Catherine Tait (8)
Bexton County Primary School

MY SHADOW

I saw a shadow like a mouse in the house.
A dark place.
It was a long thin shadow like a stick.
A dark place.
It looked like a small, little alien.
A dark place.
It came from Mars in and out of space.
A dark place.
It's only a shadow!

Peter Harrison (8)
Bexton County Primary School

THE SHADOW IN MY HOUSE

My shadow is scary.
It ran after me when I jumped into bed.
There is no light.
It looks like a battered can.
There is no light.
It was sliding down the banister.
There is no light.
My shadow follows me everywhere.
There is no light.
It looks weird, it has six fingers and his body is squashed.
There is no light.
It came from the wardrobe.
There is no light.
It's only a shadow.

Dominic Baker (7)
Bexton County Primary School

THE SHADOW

A shadow is really dull and scary.
Shadows are formed when objects are opaque.
It was really tall, scary like a fierce
monster upon my bedroom wall.
Shadows are formed when objects are opaque.
It looked like a large rugby ball with ears, arms and legs
but most of all it's really hairy indeed.
Shadows are formed when objects are opaque.
It had come in from my window and went into my bed.
Shadows are formed when objects are opaque.
It's only a shadow!

Laura Redhead (7)
Bexton County Primary School

IN A DEEP, DARK WOOD

I was in a deep, dark wood and I saw
a shadow like Robin Hood.
Not any light.
It was a straight, quite thin shape.
Not any light.
I think it was hiding behind a tree
getting ready to pounce on me!
Not any light.
At first it scared me, but then I got to know him
and made quite a good friendship.
Not any light.
Then I looked at my watch, bedtime!
Not any light.
So me and my shadow have to say goodbye,
and we'll be best friends till the day we die.
Not any light.
It's only a shadow!

David Bell (7)
Bexton County Primary School

THE STREET SHADOW

I saw a shadow of my mum and me.
A shadow is formed when things are opaque.
The shadow was tall and funny and it moved away like me.
A shadow is formed when things are opaque.
The shadow of my mum and me is like black pictures in a story book.
A shadow is formed when things are opaque.
It is very big, the shadow came from my bed the night before
and it is grey, after all it's only a shadow!

Hannah Langford (7)
Bexton County Primary School

UNTITLED

I have seen a shadow of my little dead Ratty.
It's only a shadow.
Its face looked like a bird's head.
It's only a shadow.
It looked sweet like a furry little snail.
It's only a shadow.
When she wanted food, she would jump up like a whale.
It's only a shadow.
It came from her cage, the light shone through the window.
It's only a shadow.
The shadow did what she did when she played a game.
It's only a shadow.
I miss my little Ratty.

Kate Slinger (7)
Bexton County Primary School

SHADOWS

When I woke up I saw a shadow on the floor.
My shadow is black.
It is black and big and it has funny hair.
My shadow is black.
The shadow's face is funny.
My shadow is black.
My shadow comes from a magic mountain.
My shadow is black.
It's only a shadow!

Matthew O'Brien (8)
Bexton County Primary School

MY SHADOW

I have a little shadow who hides in the shed
and then climbs upstairs in my nice warm bed.
It is you, but black.
He has a black middle like a big, huge panther
and he went upstairs for a shower.
It is you, but black.
He looks like a big, fat monster that has a case
and in his hand was the adjectives on his face.
It is you, but black.
My shadow cuts the grass every night,
and when I look at it in the morning
I jump up in fright!
He goes to the kitchen to eat once more,
the food goes straight through him
and falls upon the floor!
It is you, but black.
Eggs and beans all over the floor,
I hope he never comes any more.
It is you, but black.
Then he sings a poem which is mine you see,
and then you see him fast asleep.
It is you, but black.
It is only a shadow!

Simon Douglas (8)
Bexton County Primary School

UNTITLED

I go to bed because
My shadow is scared
It goes big and small
It looks like a troll
When it goes small
It looks like a giant
When it goes big
It comes from the sun
It's only a shadow.

Nicholas Thornley (8)
Bexton County Primary School

THE GARDEN

What can you see in the garden?
What can you see in the grass?
A butterfly shiny and busy by a flower
The snail seems to take an hour
Behind a brick a caterpillar speeding by
Up above you can you see a dragonfly?
Beneath a pot a spotty ladybird just about to fly
Crawling up a spade
An ant doesn't mind being kind
In a silky web
A spider is waiting for the dragonfly
To bring a fly
Crawling through the mud
A worm speeding by
What is in the grass?
A beetle scurrying past.

Stephanie Hough (7)
Brooklands Primary School

THE GARDEN

What can you see in the garden?
What can you see in the grass?
A millipede is busy beneath the flower pot hiding from its enemy.
A slug is slimy on a spade slithering off it.
A pond skater is speeding across a pond,
To get away from a fly that might try to eat it.
A hairy spider climbing on a rock dangling off its web.
A centipede is speedy beneath a plant pot,
Scuttling round and round.
A dragonfly is shiny,
Fluttering above a spider web and gets stuck.
A ladybird is crawling on a leaf eating it
And it's just about to fly.
A bee is buzzing just about to sting some one.
A shiny beetle is crawling up and on a person.

Rorie Sparkes (7)
Brooklands Primary School

THE GARDEN

What can you see in the garden?
What can you see in the grass?
One hairy spider hanging from a web beside a spade.
One little ant crawling around a brick.
One spotty ladybird climbing up a stem
with six little speedy legs.
One dragonfly flying round a flower
for now it's getting dizzy.
One colourful butterfly learning how to fly.
One little bat hanging upside down in a dark bush.
One shiny beetle crawling on a leaf.

Gabriella Farrell (7)
Brooklands Primary School

THE GARDEN

What can you see in the garden?
What can you see in the grass?
A big hairy spider settling down to snooze.
A busy ant finding food near a plant.
One big bee collecting pollen from each of the plants.
A speedy worm hiding under a brick from its enemy.
One ladybird scuttling up and down a spade.
One dragonfly lying near the larva.
A lazy grasshopper trying to do first jump.
A pond skater skating on a pond backwards and forwards.
A butterfly flying above the long grass.
A big fly trying to get out of a spider's web.
A caterpillar getting out of its cocoon but it was too fat
and got stuck.
An earwig trying to avoid a person's foot.
A glow worm glowing in the dark.

Rahul Chattopadhyay (7)
Brooklands Primary School

THE GARDEN

What can you see in the garden?
What can you see in the grass?
A spider with hairy legs above the plant pot making a spider's web.
A caterpillar with spots on a brick sliding down.
I saw a slug in the garden.
It was slimy.
It was above the flower, it was slithering.
One ant who is busy behind a spade digging a hole.
On the top of a pool one speedy pond skater sliding quickly by.

Chris Pugh (7)
Brooklands Primary School

THE GARDEN

What can you see in the garden?
What can you see in the grass?
A big hairy spider in the middle of a web.
A grasshopper in the grass jumping around.
On the ground an ant finding food.
A busy bee collecting pollen from a flower.
The herd of shiny beetles will make a crowd
To make a nest in the ground.
Tadpoles swimming in a pool
And on top a pond skater cool.
A big fly trying to get away from the spider's web.
A caterpillar getting out of his cocoon
But he's too fat and he's stuck.
An earwig trying to avoid a person.
A glow worm glowing in the dark.

Daniel Corker (6)
Brooklands Primary School

THE GARDEN

What can you see in the garden?
What can you see in the grass?
I can see a long caterpillar having a little snack.
While a spotty ladybird is busy in the grass,
A bird is looking for worms
And the worms just squirm.
One pond skater skating by,
While a spider is waiting for a fly.
One beautiful butterfly flying in bluest sky.
One little ant crawling round a brick.
Five shiny beetles just passing by.

Megan McCrudden (7)
Brooklands Primary School

THE GARDEN

What can you see in the garden?
What can you see in the grass?
A beautiful butterfly flying in the sky.
A little tiny ant crawling around the path.
A big hairy spider weaving a web.
A slimy, slimy slug sleeping under a stone.
A bumblebee busy making honey.
A little spotty ladybird nibbling on a flower.
A black shiny beetle running round and round.
A pond skater skating on the pond.
A lazy worm sleeping in the soil.
A jumping grasshopper hopping in the grass.
A very busy wasp sitting in a flower.
A lot of tadpoles in a pond.
A blue and green dragonfly flying above the ground.
A hairy caterpillar slowly crawling on a leaf.
A million woodlice under a brick . . .

Stephanie Tait (7)
Brooklands Primary School

ANGER!

Boil up like a kettle,
explode like a bomb,
get ticked off like a clock,
stamp down stairs like an elephant,
run outside as fast as a cheetah,
swing on a tree like a monkey,
break of branches like a lumber jack,
climb down trees like a falling snail,
become mad, really mad like a dog.

Daniel Murray (10)
Brooklands Primary School

NIGHT-TIME

The golden chariot disappears
I shut the curtains
I switch out the light
I climb into my cosy bed
I feel safe and secure
Soon I am in a deep sleep
I am awakened by the sound of footsteps
It's only my dad downstairs
I walk to the window
I open the window
I see a tree
It looks like a man waving his hands
I climb back into bed
Look at the door that's hanging open
The dressing gown hanging from my door looks like a ghost
I'm shivering with fright
The flowers on my window sill look like the heads of skeletons
I go to sleep again
Next thing I know is the velvet cover is disappearing
The golden chariot is coming up for the day ahead.

Rebecca Donaldson (11)
Brooklands Primary School

CHEETAH

Creeping, crawling, ready to pounce
He has seen his prey
Shining teeth
Graceful but powerful paws

A splendid, spotted, soft coat
Gleaming in the sun
The gold and black, a blur as it runs

Eyes are a blazing, burning furnace

Slowly, smoothly
He creeps closer, closer
Squatting near the ground

Pounce
It has caught the prey
Falls down
Eats
Then satisfaction.

Harry Pettener (11)
Brooklands Primary School

THE ANGRY SEA

The sea is a vicious wild dog,
drooling, roaring, rolling stones everywhere.
The green pollution oozed across the ocean.
Everywhere whirlpools sunk away right down,
screaming, vicious, crunching of the stones,
waves turning black and grey.
You can hear whistling wind howling all over the ocean.
Stones tossing, stones cracked in half against the rock.
The angry sky turned all black and grey.
A sea foaming, monstrous waves,
lightning struck across the sky.
The power of the raging waves.
Jaws are grinding together.
Sea squeals, sways and belches.
The beast now is leaving.
People are calm.
The beast has run out of power.
Gone into the ocean, but will be back.

Ryan Green (11)
Brooklands Primary School

MY BARKING DOG

At night when I climb into bed
My mum comes up and tucks me in tight.
I get out a scary book.
I read and read until my eyes start to water.
When I pull my pillow down.
My head goes down.
There isn't a sound.
Tonight I could not get to sleep.
My dog was barking.
I got out of bed.
Tiptoed to the toilet.
There I saw my dog barking
Because a fox was eating his dinner.
I walked back.
I climbed into bed.
Soon I was fast asleep.

Jenny Yates (10)
Brooklands Primary School

WALKING WAVES

The sea is like a horse.
When angry he bucks and bites your feet.
He gallops onto the sand.

His mane is mangled, black and white.
Whipping the sky.
His little white friends are swimming in the sea.

They make white marks in the sea.
Angrily they whinny the water.
Obeying their master's cries.

He is tired now.
His white friends are weeping in the water.
They are sad that their friend has to go back to his stable.
Deep into the darkness until dawn.

Alex Robinson (11)
Brooklands Primary School

AT NIGHT

I get into my cosy warm bed
And start to doze off.
The bed starts to shake
I sprint downstairs.
'Mum, Mum there's something under my bed.'
She comes up and nothing is there.
I start to snuggle down in my bed.
I dream that an alien has come and captured me.
I looked at the window and saw a hand.
I looked harder and it was no longer there.
It was just a leaf from the tree.
At the door there was a person walking to me.
It was dark, dull and gloomy.
The thing was coming nearer and nearer.
The moon shone brightly on the moving sight.
It was my dressing gown.
I settled back to sleep in my cosy bed.
The sun came out.
I realised it was all in my imagination.

Amy Ainsworth (11)
Brooklands Primary School

ANGER

I run upstairs
My face is like a burst plum
My eyes are narrow
I clench my teeth and screw my nose
I feel like a runaway train
I could run, run
I feel like a burst bomb
A steamed potato
I call my family names
I kick and punch and shout
Scream and stamp
When I've finished shouting
I cool and say sorry.

Jonathan Richards (11)
Brooklands Primary School

ANGER

I'm a raving lunatic
I want to throw everything everywhere
I'm like a button ready to pop off someone's trousers
I feel like smashing the whole house down

I've got a boiling hot red face
I am ill tempered
I'm saying things I don't mean
I'm a bull ready to charge at anyone I see

Slowly I calm down and think about what I've done
I was so stupid
I can't believe it.

Andrew Wynne (11)
Brooklands Primary School

THE ANGRY SEA

The sea is like a fiery dragon
Just waiting to explode
With death awaiting around the corner

An angry sea tossing and turning
Pounding on the rocks
Just like an angry beast
A cascade of colour in the sky
A whistling, raging sea
Smashing upon the sand

The sea is calming down
Just like George killed the dragon
The sky a beautiful red colour
Like a last flame of fire.

Michael Broad (11)
Brooklands Primary School

THE LION

A meat eater, proud and powerful,
King of the jungle, strong and fierce.
The fur is yellowy,
Smooth and has a lovely gloss,
Silky, soft and gentle.
Eyes sharp and gleaming red,
Staring at his prey.
Moving slowly and steady,
Creeping towards his tasty prey.
Then fast he pounces,
Grabs the prey with his sharp and greedy teeth.
Blood spurts out, it dribbles down his chin.

Rebecca Gee (11)
Brooklands Primary School

THE BLACK SEA

The sea is like a leopard resting during day.
Hunting all through the lonely night.
The beautiful moon gives off a lustrous white light.
It reflects off its black sea - like fur:
Little puny waves of hair still exist from when the enchanting
beast cleaned itself from before.

Night falls, colossal clouds.
Stomp in like gazelle prancing through a golden field.
Suddenly two clouds collide like two bucks fighting for a mate.
The crashing sound awakens the beast.

Slowly, the beast gets up.
He begins to jump.
The puny little waves in his hairs turned into monster waves.
More clouds come storming in.
The leopard like sea was now furiously swaying back and forth.
Spitting out foam like drool which is washed onto the seashore.

Morning breaks out.
The beast begins to die down.
He will be reborn when night falls!

Peter Symaniw (11)
Brooklands Primary School

THE ANGRY EVENING

I slam shut the unlucky kitchen door,
With the power of a Roman Gladiator.
I scream 'I hate you parents'
With the full strength of my weary lungs.

I pound my way up the dying stairs
Like a herd of rampaging elephants.
Steam shoots off my hot, red, burning ears
You could fry an egg on my forehead.

I kick my bedroom door open with incredible vigour,
The pain of the kick mixes in with the pain of my anger.
The clang of the handle of the door against the wall,
Echoes round my suffering house.

Thoughts of my poor family come into my head,
I stop and think about why I am doing all this terrorisation
And destruction.

I slowly walk down the poor stairs,
Back to my war zone downstairs of my house.
I apologise to my parents and my brother,
All is then forgotten for the day.

Chris Rushton (11) & Lauren Brown (10)
Brooklands Primary School

THE ANGRY SEA

The angry sea is like a vicious lion.
Crashing waves, smashing onto the shore.
White horses escaping from the lion.
He is slowly devouring the sea,
Moving the pebbles under his feet.

The dark purple skies.
Whistling wind.
Booming thunder.
Crackling lightning.
Lightning, flashing across the sky.

At last the lion gets tired.
He goes back into the sea
And into its den
And leaves the people safe
Until another day . . .

Stephie Knowles (11)
Brooklands Primary School

THE LION

The lion is the king of the jungle hunting its prey.
His shiny, soft coat and fierce, ferocious face
looking at its prey.

Its fur gleaming in the sun.
The golden gleam in it shines out.
It sparkles like the moon.

Its eyes are red, staring at its prey.
Flaming like the sun staring still at its prey
ready to pounce any second.

The lion moves slyly, slowly and steadily.
Quietly it moves towards its prey.
Quietly and slowly then all of a sudden
it pounces high up into the air, on its prey
and now the lion is proud.

Rachael Gregg (11)
Brooklands Primary School

THE BIG CAT

The proud, graceful meat eater
Was strolling along into the vast jungle,
Ready, alert to find his juicy prey.
The meat eater was resting
Its magical skin gleaming in this bright sunlight.
A soft, thick eerie yellow black coat
Warm as ever.
The meat eater jumps up in surprise,
Sees his prey in front of him.
His long quiet stride through the sharp grass,
Concentrating on the animal
Never taking his eyes off,
Ready to pounce on the animal,
Creeping towards looking curious out for danger.
Moments later
A loud roar of happiness from the leopard.
Runs to somewhere to hide.
The meat eater as proud as can be.
Bright red blood dribbling down his chin,
Ripping parts apart.

Natasha Danson (11)
Brooklands Primary School

ANGRY

My face went all red,
my head was going to burst like a volcano.
My whole body was full of steam.
My eyes were red with fire.

I stamped upstairs
and slammed the door.
I threw my teddy on the floor.
Ripped my pillow up, I was so angry.

Soon I calmed down and went downstairs
to apologise to my mum.
When I got upstairs
I said to myself
why did I get so angry?

Hannah Cordiner (11)
Brooklands Primary School

ANGER!

My face is about to pop like a balloon
My blood is sizzling up
Flames are coming out of my mouth.

My eyes are about to come out of their socket
I feel like a lion roaring
My face is bright red
One inch of my face is ready to pop.

I'm pounding up the stairs like a kangaroo
I slam my door ripping my toys, medals on the floor
My room is like a tip.

Robert McKie (10)
Brooklands Primary School

THE ANGRY SEA

The dreary, drab, dull sky overlooks the furious beast of a sea,
tearing the desolate rock away, battering the soft sand.
It eats the land like a raging, rabid blue monster,
ripping the rocks apart with no problems.
Its winds howl through seaside towns.

The sea throws the anchored boats around like matchsticks
flooding the land, taking lives by the dozen.
It tears up cliffs, whirling the rocks round and round.

Suddenly the dazzling sun drives the pouring rain and roaring wind
back, calming the sea, sending it back to its deep lair.
The dishevelled beach and misplaced rocks regain their former
places, more lives lost at sea have been added to the total.

Kieran Widdowson (11)
Brooklands Primary School

THE SEA

The sea is like an angry bull
charging backwards
and forwards.
Raving at his enemy.

The bull is charging at the rocks,
taking bits as it leaves.
He spits them out
as he goes back for more.

The wild whistling of the wind,
calms down now.
The angry bull gets tired,
and falls asleep.

Hannah McKie (10)
Brooklands Primary School

NIGHT

The day is slowly disappearing,
the moon is taking over.
The jet black sky is coming to take the blue sky away.

The stars are twinkling more than ever.
In my room I can see lots of shadows,
like the leaves on the tree,
like hands coming to get me!

I snuggle down into my safe, warm bed,
feeling a lot safer.
I hope that the night goes faster.

Into a deep sleep,
then the next door cat at the front door.
I hope that night goes faster.
A gust of wind comes in my bedroom.

My dressing gown look like a ghost with a hood on.
My cupboard looks like it's
going to get me!

I creep to my window and look outside,
it is a very windy night.
The street has not got many lights.

Dawn is appearing.
The sun coming up and the night
is disappearing.
The night is battling to stay up.

Stephanie Megson (10)
Brooklands Primary School

NIGHT-TIME

The day is slowly disappearing,
a pitch black sheet covers the earth
it takes over from the sun and the blue sky.

The stars are glistening.
A big ball shining more than ever in the sky.
My room is shining and full of light.
The leaves look like hands waving in the wind,
coming to take me!

I snuggle down,
secure and cosy in bed
and dream about what will happen tomorrow.
I fall straight to sleep.

I hear a frightening noise,
and jump up and start to shiver,
I can hear footsteps,
coming towards me!
The door opens
I can see a figure,
I think it's a monster!
Phew! it's only my mum,
and she tells me to get to sleep.

I wake up and hear a noise,
this time it's a nice noise,
it's the birds.
The sun and moon have had another fight.
The sun has won again.

Chris Cameron (11)
Brooklands Primary School

BONFIRE PARTY

Children running about everywhere, a smoky feeling in the air.
People are handing tickets in and paying to get in.
The smell of hot dogs is in the air, smiling faces are everywhere.
Everybody wrapped up warm.

The bonfire is blazing, a dazzling sight. It is getting hotter by
                                 the minute.
The orange, yellow and red of the flames dance up and down.
It's nearly time to start.

Fantastic fireworks whoosh here and there, showing their bright
                                  colours off.
Everyone says ooh, everyone says aah, as the fireworks fly on by.
The beautiful Catherine wheel whooshes, the bangers bang.
The rockets rocket into the night sky.

At the end everyone walks home into the night.
At the end of the bonfire party.

Amy Mullen (11)
Brooklands Primary School

THE ANGRY SEA

The sea is like a tiger
as it pounds on the rocks
All bits go flying into the air
like birds flying in the sky

Suddenly bang
it's like the tiger banging his foot
on the bottom of the sea
The lightning is his glaring eyes

The sea is whirling
like the tiger biting into his
prey, tossing and turning

Suddenly it starts to slow down
it's getting tired
it dies down.

Sarah Doyle (10)
Brooklands Primary School

ANGER!

Red faced,
Purple nosed,
Bulging eyeballs,
Itching toes.
Volcano erupting,
Runaway train,
Fire bursting,
It's happening again,
Daring,
Tearing,
Thump and throw,
Everything's broken,
I don't care,
So
I am ready to go out now,
I open the door,
Sorry mum I won't do it any more.

Edward Prophet (11)
Brooklands Primary School

ANGER

I am a volcano erupting.
Throwing a tantrum.
Swearing.
My blood is sizzling like sausages in a pan.
Steam is coming out of my ears.
As red as a ripe tomato.
I rip up all my T-shirts.
Screaming.
Fumes coming from my hair.
I stamp up the stairs.
Slam my bedroom door.
Shouting and swearing.
Throwing my teddies about.
I start calming down, lie on my bed.
Think about what I've done.
I start tidying my bedroom.

Jessica Heywood (10)
Brooklands Primary School

THE ANGRY SEA

Darkening clouds cover the dingy sky.
The fierce waves assaulting and attacking anything in its path.
Roaming the open sea ready to pounce and clinging to everything.

The chief of all villains elevating the wild ocean.
Rocks clashing and colliding with the ferocious beast.
An untamed monster flooding the land.
Chaos everywhere, waves rolling as it forms a frothy foam.
Boats sunk and destroyed below the murky ocean depths.
All life forms *dead!*

Amanda Cashin (11)
Brooklands Primary School

THE LION

The lion slyly appears
Out from the bushes
It glares straight ahead
Concentrated eyes glared at his prey
His big bushy tail like it was paralysed.

Glossy, thick, warm, soft fur
Gleaming in the sun
The colour of his fur was camouflaged
with the sunlight
Only his mane was distinctive
His golden fur shone
His eyes are staring
Fixed on his scared prey
Eyes stretched as far as they will go

The lion gets into a pouncing
Position, crouches down low
All of a sudden he leaps out
And pounces on his prey
Grabs it and carries it in its mouth . . .
Blood dripping down the lion's mouth
Gobbling up its prey
Tearing it apart then licking his lips
Scraping up the remains
The lion's eyes are beginning
To get weary looking
He slowly walks away
Tired but satisfied.

Lucie Buchan (11)
Brooklands Primary School

ANGER

I stomped upstairs
And slammed the door
My eyes bulged out
I went dark red
My nose scrunched up
Out of my ears came boiled steam.

I felt like a murderer
Or maybe a mugger
A volcano erupting
A bomb ready to go *bang*
A rugby player going on and on.

I ripped the pillow
Jumped on my teddy
I threw my books across the room
I stomped, I swore
I screamed and danced
I kicked the wardrobe
And hurt my toe
Suddenly I stopped
I decided to calm down
I had said things I did not mean
I went downstairs
And said sorry
To mum and dad.

Matthew Randall (11)
Brooklands Primary School

ANGER

I felt furious, like a wild animal.
How dare he!
That was it.
That was that.
I stamped and swore!
I could punch him!
I did.
Anger took over me.
Bang! Slam!
Down went the knife and fork.
Bang went the door.
My head was ready to take off like a spaceship!
I screamed, I cried.
I swore, I yelled.
Stomp, stomp, stomp!
Stomp, stomp, stomp!
I stormed upstairs like a Mig 21.
Crash!
The door was blown open by an angry fist.
I was so angry, I could rip the door off its hinges.
The tape was turned up to my full volume of rage.
Lucy my cat came on the bed.
I stroked her.
She licked my hand.
I wondered should I have done that?
Why?
I went down and said sorry to my cousins.
But it was his fault after all.

Jill Thomason (11)
Brooklands Primary School

THE EMPTY HOUSE

The rusty gate in a crumpled heap on cracked path,
The decrepit gatepost, nearly falling to pieces,
I follow the path, crumbling like an ancient city,
The garden like a graveyard for plants,
The old tree stopped blossoming eight years ago.
The horrible colour carried on throughout the garden,
The slates on the roof cracked like a ripped page.
Crash!
A slate off the roof smashed into tiny pieces.
I shifted towards the door,
As I touched it, the door crumbled into tiny pieces.

I shuffled through the door,
Watching my step all the way, eeeeeek!
A floorboard creaked beneath my foot,
The very wide winding stairs shielded by a blanket of dust.
I shifted up the winding stairs,
Quietly I opened the door
And from the bottom of the stairs
A blood curdling scream was heard,
And the slamming of a door.
Sprinting down the stairs
I nipped through the kitchen
And hurdled out of the back door,
Giving one last look at the house
I quickly ran home.

Michael Heap (10)
Brooklands Primary School

THE ANGRY SEA

The savage thunder beast arises from his deep dreamless doze,
which wakes his vast powered brother, god of lightning.
The dim clouds creep over the misty sky like a black velvet gown.
Gleeful children are killed unless they join their terrified parents
inside their houses.
A magnificent storm is on the way.

Immense waves reek havoc on defenceless rocks.
The blood thirsty creature of the storm destroys anything
which crosses his path.
The pounding noise of the deafening thunder splits the dim
sky into millions of puny, sombre pieces.
The angry sea claws ships down to the bottom of its murky depths.

The beast of thunder goes back to his dozy, dreamless slumber.
The god of lightning drifts back to his home to replenish his power.
There are numerous ship wrecks to add to the tally.
Hundreds of lives have been claimed by the grim reaper at the
bottom of this sea.
Joyful children return to the beaches, people start mourning
the loss of their loved ones.
The sky changes colour, the sun comes out.

David Tait (10)
Brooklands Primary School

BONFIRE NIGHT

People are dashing around, the smell of hot dogs and burgers excites me.
The people have warm coats and gloves on, the sky is dark and the moon glows brightly in the sky.

The bonfire crackles burning wood, thick smoke rises from the scorching flames which dance on the fire, golden sparks come raining out. The fire is wild!

Now the fireworks are being lit! The crowd stops silent as the match is struck, it lowers and then sparks start spurting out! They zoom out like blazing stars with golden sparks, the crowd watches in excitement! Then the rocket roars up, flares of magical sparks are still spurting out rapidly! Then bang! Showers of tremendous fiery wild stars explode out! Light bursts out in red, yellow, blue, white, golden and silver! Then it goes completely out of sight, the excitement has disappeared but it will come back when the next firework is lit.

Then later, the fireworks are finished and the bonfire slowly shrinks, all that is left is the remains of the wood, the black and white ashes are still. A shimmer of smoke still is flowing out. White plastic cups and towels are lying on the ground. People walk back home and now the whole place is quiet, but it was a great bonfire night!

Allan Whatmough (11)
Brooklands Primary School

THE COLD NIGHT

When it's cold outside and
There's nowhere to hide,
The day disappears,
The night becomes clear.

I wrap myself up warm.
The window smashes! *Crash!*
I get sucked out, into
The deserted air.

The graveyard appears.
Out comes a man
Who is all sad and scary.

He looks at me with his
Dark red eyes
And I'm telling you
It gave me quite a surprise.

I dropped my teddy and
Ran out of the door.
I went running faster,
And faster across the floor.

He's chasing me
Like a devil from the sea.

Then a familiar figure appears,
It's a lady!
With short, dark hair.
It's my *mum!*

Elizabeth Burgess (10)
Brooklands Primary School

BONFIRE NIGHT

The bonfire night is beaming with rage as its
sparkling glow is going up into the pitch night.
You can hear the spitting of the bonfire blazing
on through the night as you walk through the gates.
Everyone was wrapped up on this freezing cold night.

With its spectacular, scorching flames, golden
as autumn leaves, it's like a fountain of sparks
flying out of tremendous blaze. You can see
it just rising into the dull sky as the gloomy
night passes on. It's like a dragon roaring with
rage, spitting out its scorching hot fire.

The fireworks are like showers of crimson
colours rising then exploding into the sky,
as colourful as a bird's feather. The brilliant
golden glow makes me shut my eyes because
it is that golden. The beautiful, bright bangers
make scattered showers of bright colours.

At last the scorching hot fire is dissolving
down to heaps of ashes. Everybody leaving very
happily because of the entertainment of the
fireworks and the bonfire. Lots of litter on
the ground for some poor people to pick it all up.

Matthew Guy (11)
Brooklands Primary School

THE STORM

The cloudless sky of the day dims as the menace of the night
                                                          approaches.
The rampant rain was dabbling out of the haunting, ebony sky.
The black devil approaches, aroused from his devil's den,
intent on spreading chaos over the blackened beach again.
The devil's magic spell is carried out.

The fatal waves flood the desolate wooden beach huts.
The wind and rain slash the solid, silver rocks
and the huge, defensive sea wall.
The fringed, freezing sand is covered by his cold black hand of death.

The devil's spell is wearing off.
Planks of rotting, splintering wood bob around in the rippling water.
The watery sun slowly comes out.
The golden shimmering sand is recovered.
The devil slips away into his deep dark cavern awaiting the day
when he can reappear again.

Pamela Lingham (11)
Brooklands Primary School

ANGER

How could she do this to me?
Is this as nice as she can be?
I think I will disown that devil,
Storming up to the next level.
Crashing and thudding all the way,
Why couldn't they be nice and gay?
At the top and through the door,
Running around like a boar.
Smashing and crashing all my things,
Around my room a bouncy ball pings.
Bouncing around on my bed,
Making the wall hit my head.
Will my blood vessels ever pop?
Will I ever stop?
I finally realise I am wrong,
I run out of the house and
'Ding, dong!'
There I have a new beginning,
My world has finally stopped spinning.

Kate Higginbottom (11)
Brooklands Primary School

BEDTIME

The sun sets in the sky,
My mum says 'Bedtime.'
All the colours glisten away,
The only colours left are black and grey.

The moon twinkles in the sky
Showing off gleaming high.
No one listens to him now,
The moon is there high and proud.

I snuggle up tight and aglow,
Thinking of all the things below.
I know I'm safe in my bed,
I snuggle up tight with my Ted.

I woke up with a cold sweat,
Is my Ted still in my bed?
I keep on hearing all these things,
Plops, bangs and also dings.

I look around the room with fright,
Looking at all the things of night.
My dressing gown looks like a gloomy ghost
And the lampshade looks like a bat.

The dawn appears and all my fright
Has gone away into the night.
The monsters hide out and about,
Yippee, until another night.

David Cawley (11)
Brooklands Primary School

THE STORM

The grey, gloomy sky open up above
The Satan of the sea turned the soft, velvety depths into
a roaring barbaric wilderness.
The clouds grumbled angrily.
Whoosh! Went a flash of lightning.
Whoosh! Screamed the savage thunder.
The furious waves collided rigidly with the rocks.
A brutal whirlpool forms in the centre of the black,
lethal sea, pulling in boats.
The wrecked boat spins and turns.
Round and round, into the shattered and destroyed boat which
disappears along with the last glimmer of light.
Houses are flooded.
The raging sea kills innocent people,
who are screaming for their lives,
but their screams are no match for the murderous, hungry sea.
The terrifying sky's howls die down, and its darkness begins to crack.
A tiny ray of light hits the now calm sea.
One last wave floats into the rocks and the storm is over (for now!)

Paul Handforth (11)
Brooklands Primary School

THE ANGRY SEA

The sky opened and the lightning bolted out.
The storm started and the sea struck out.
Sea is evil, grabbing everything in sight,
Like a ravenous, raving monster rolling onto the rocks.

The angry sea throws itself over the boats.
The fish get tossed and turned in the sea,
Drowning anything in its way,
Soaking anything on the land with a salty spray.
Most of the fish are dead.
The seabeds have been tossed and turned.
Plants have been torn in half by the power.

The monster stopped and went away.
The sea died down.
You could see the wrecked ships.
More people were drowned by the monster.
Hopefully the monster won't go hungry
For a few more days.

Andrew Ireland (11)
Brooklands Primary School

THE EMPTY HOUSE

I pass it . . .
The *dead house.*
Something pulls me towards its gate,
Silently swaying in the breeze.
I walk, mesmerised towards its rusty, crumbling gate,
disintegrating in my fingers.
I silently saunter, scared, towards its holed and gaping windows,
through the garden, wasted and sad.
There is no door,
just a hole.
I creep in, stirring only mice,
sending a shiver up my spine.

As I amble up the warped, distorted stairs,
I hear a twisted, terrifying, terrible scream.
At that moment, the curtains flap in my face.
I look with horror upon a grave outside.
I fly into a panic, throwing myself down the stairs,
the scream following me, enveloping me.

I burst from the house, run through the garden,
the plants bonding me to the house.
I yank free, not looking back.
I never want to look upon the *dead house* again.

Meredydd Jones (10)
Brooklands Primary School

THE DARK NIGHT

The sun goes down,
The moon comes out,
I was going to bed,
When I heard a shout.

A blood curdling scream,
I fall out of bed,
I land on the floor,
And bump my head.

I walk to the window,
I take a big leap,
As I open the curtains,
And take a small peep.

I look through the window,
To the other house,
I hear a small squeak,
But it's only a mouse.

I wake up the next day,
It was only a dream,
At least I think it was,
Or so it may seem.

Mark Watson (11)
Brooklands Primary School

I'M SO ANGRY!

I'm so, so mad I could explode into a thousand pieces
Like a steaming volcano ready to erupt.
I'm really, really angry now, I see *red!*
I scream as loud as I can,
Like an angry dragon breathing fire.

I'm steaming up like an old, rusty kettle on the boil,
And stamping up the stairs like a herd of elephants.
Thump, thump, thump!
I can't explain how angry I really am or I will burst.

I slam open my bedroom door, *bang, crash!*
Everything shakes and things fall of my walls.
I take all my covers off my bed and jump on it.
I scream so loud, my ears pop.

I lie on my bed and look up at the plain, dry ceiling,
And listen to the silence which is broken by the wind,
Whistling through the dying trees.
I listen carefully to my conscience.

I go down the creeping stairs and say to myself
'I was so stupid'
And think of myself, why did I do all those things?

Kate Gibson (11)
Brooklands Primary School

BONFIRE NIGHT

Bonfire night is here today,
the bonfire burns as the fireworks play.
The guy's on the top sizzling away,
on top of the rubbish we piled day by day.
Poor old guy not made for much,
to be put on a bonfire then sizzled up.
Children laughing and chasing the sparks
that come off the bonfire and leave little marks.
Now for the fireworks, the first one's a *bang,*
so loud I have to cover my ears with my hands.
Shooting stars zoom through the air,
then suddenly disappear.
Time for the Catherine wheel as it whirls around,
sparks fly off and fall to the ground.
Next ones are whistlers, what a lovely sound,
but dissolves in the air and doesn't hit the ground.
What a brilliant time, such a wonderful sight,
can't wait 'til next bonfire night.

Ella Dore (11)
Brooklands Primary School

THE STORM

The thick dangerous vicious clouds storm
over the rippled sea.
Suddenly, unexpectedly the god of the clouds,
the golden lion appears throwing an enormous
bolt of dangerous lightning which comes
ripping down to the calm milky sea.
Swiftly and magically constructs a tiny ride,
Into a huge fire, like raging waves,
Gushing against small, innocent fishing boats,
Wrapping the small boats into huge whirlwinds,
Sucking the fishing boats to the sandy bottom of the sea,
Seizing the boats to the sharp, white cliffs of Dover.
It grasps proudly, fish and boats, magicing them to the
bottom of the deep blue sea.
The angry lion of the clouds disappears.
The sun peeps out behind the dark black cloud.
It calms the rough, blue sea into only a ripple as the storm ends.
But it has still sucked the lives of hundreds.

Fern McDonald (10)
Brooklands Primary School

FRIGHTENING NIGHT

The candle is out,
Grown-ups are asleep,
But little children sit,
And cry.

The night and the dark have come once more,
To scare little children out of their wits.
Ghosts and creaks creep into the house,
To scare little children a little bit more.

There's darkness everywhere,
In the airing cupboard and in the hall,
Little children scream and shout,
But the darkness muffles all noise.

Ghosts creep around the house,
As quiet as a mouse,
Creaks start creaking everywhere,
Frightening the stairs.

The moon and stars laugh,
At little children with white faces,
Shivering in their beds,
Pulling the sheet over their heads.

Then children run to their mums,
Ghosts and creaks creep away,
The sun comes up,
Light appears.

Helen Monaghan (11)
Brooklands Primary School

ANGER

I slammed the door behind me,
Leaving those annoying things behind,
My face is hot and sizzling,
Blood is boiling like a fireball inside me,
Stampeding up the stairs like a herd of wildebeests,
As I advance to my bedroom door,
I feel like a sourpuss,
My door bursts open with a great big thud,
I'm a raving lunatic!
Screaming and yelling out of my window,
As I glance over to my worn out teddy,
I leap on the bed with a great big *boing!*
Snuggling into his soft, pink fur,
I became calm once more.

Natalie Dent (11)
Brooklands Primary School

THE ANGRY SEA

The gloomy, dull sky swarms towards the rocky beach,
The frothy waves start lapping onto each other.
Evil clouds gather together to plan revenge,
A hideous beast emerges from the powerful sea.
His swollen body crashes down onto the rocks,
Thunder booms, the storm had begun.

Ravenous waves slam down onto rocky mountains,
A boat gets thrown up and up and down.
The dreaded devil throws himself, thrashing it with his lion mane,
The repulsive creature leaps from the water like a king with his crown.
The sky clears, the clouds float away,
The monster is nowhere to be seen.
Children come with their rubber rings,
The storm had come and been.

Wendy Baranowska (11)
Brooklands Primary School

I WONDER WHY

I wonder why the nights are pitch black, dark?
Scary creatures creep into the park.
I wonder why the night is not light like day?
Foxes are on their nightly prowl around the streets.
I wonder why the nights are gloomy and grey?
While hooting owls fly around and search for their prey.
I wonder why the nights are freezing cold?
Snowflakes glistening on the road.
I wonder why the nights are startling, scary?
With me shivering under the covers.
I wonder why the nights are long and lengthy?
I wait patiently for the light to come.
I wonder why the nights are glum and gloomy?
Dismal, drab and dull.
I wonder why the night is night,
and why it gives me a frightening fright?
I wonder why I will never know,
will I, who knows?

Jenny Jones (10)
Brooklands Primary School

ANGER

I'm raging, really raging.
Why do people always take it out on me?
I close my eyes.
I can see red, raving red before me.
It's not fair!

I stomp noisily up the stairs like a heffalump!
Making a point that I am really mad.
As I get to the top of the stairs,
I push open the wooden door.
I am inside,
I slam the door so hard that it nearly falls off its hinges!

I'm exasperated.
I pick up my feather pillow and punch it.
Then I have a pillow fight with the wall.
Now there are feathers everywhere.
Why have I done this?
Flopping down on the bed, I pick up my beanbag bear Jim,
I hug him till he is squashed.

As I think my mum comes in to comfort me.
She asked me why there were feathers everywhere.
I told her why and she laughed.
After that she helped to restuff my pillows.
Why did I do this, why?

Sarah Everton (11)
Brooklands Primary School

ALL HALLOWS EVE

The night of the spirits,
When the moon is round,
Werewolves can sometimes be found.
Under the trees, in the bushes
When you go out the cold wind whooshes.

Ghosts at night come in the darkness,
They are black, cold and heartless.
At night-time shadows dare,
To scare you, frighten you, are they there?

Things that go bump in the night,
Can give you an awful fright.
Sometimes they are really scary,
Toads, bats and spiders hairy.
Do you dream of all these things?
If you do you might be wary.

Vampires that can drink your blood,
Do you believe I think you should.
Dancing goblins by the fire,
When you are scared you perspire.
Skeletons have bones that crackle,
Shaky, quakes and that rattles.

All Hallows Eve please rest in peace,
Because when you go out *don't*
Haunt *me!*

Charlotte Royle (11)
Brooklands Primary School

MY FURIOUS ANGRY RAGE

The steam inside me feels as though it's
going to blow like a deadly grenade.
I am furious at my mum and dad,
the two people who make me mad.
I scream and shout, pound and ball
knowing me I'd knock down a wall.
I burst into a deadly temper and pound up
the stairs on each step I sounded like a
5000 kg weight dropped from a skyscraper
only to kill anyone who gets in my way.
I open my door, run, take a flying leap and
land on my bed.
Throw my pillows and just about breathe
fire like an angry dragon.
I could use my brain and rip down
my curtains down and parachute out
and run away then they'll be sorry.
I lie down, my fiery eyes get put out and
I start thinking about how much I overheated.
I go down, wipe away my tears and apologise.

David Gray (11)
Brooklands Primary School

HAPPINESS

Happiness is peach,
it tastes like ice-cream,
and smells like the pollen on the flowers.
Happiness looks like smiling children,
and sounds like giddy babies on a beach.
Happiness feels like a big, big smile
upon your face.

Daniel Sweeney (10)
Firs Primary School

GOODBYE SUMMER, HELLO AUTUMN

Goodbye my beautiful summer days
when I could stay out late and have
a suntan all the time. I won't be
drinking cool juice anymore, I'll be
gulping down steaming hot tea, clutching
my warm cosy blanket and gazing out of
the steamed up window.
At night when you want to go to sleep you
get a fuzzy tingle in your feet. The fire
gives a click as it warms up and you can
see the moonlight shining through the
window as you drift off into a warm cosy
sleep. When you wake in the morning you can
see water trickling down the window. It's all
blurry outside and as you look ahead you
can see smoke pumping out the chimney tops.

Louise Pennington (11)
Firs Primary School

ANGER

Anger is red.
It tastes like lava from a volcano.
It smells like a smoking fire.
It looks like a bomb exploding in your head.
Anger sounds like a death scream.
Anger feels like a twister spinning around
in your head.

Lee Hulse (11)
Firs Primary School

GOODBYE SUMMER, HELLO AUTUMN

Goodbye shining light of summer,
your shining is done.
Autumn's crunching season is just beginning.
May your exotic smells soothe our bodies.
May your blinding colours surprise all our hearts.
May your guiding path guide us slowly and discreetly
to the mild, cold of the biting winter.
Soon we shall be at the foot of winter.

Autumn has finally clawed its way through
the path of summer and stolen everything it holds.
Its raging hand has flashed new life into the path
of summer and has taken summer's place.
Its great power has put new insects and animals
into the place of summer's path.

Lee Bolland (10)
Firs Primary School

ANGER

Anger is red.
It tastes like a lump of coal stuck in your throat.
It smells like a raging fire and it looks like a tall
building being thrown to the ground.
Anger sounds like a death scream and it feels
like fire thrashing through your body.

Christopher Bird (10)
Firs Primary School

GOODBYE SUMMER, HELLO AUTUMN

I say goodbye to you summer
I'll see you again next year
I'll remember all the brilliant things I did
with the brightness of your glory

I welcome the breeze of you autumn
You blow the colourful leaves
off the beautiful trees
You go all bald without any glimmer
of the leaves

I welcome you back sensational summer
We missed your daylight last year
We missed our days out
and now you've come again for our joy.

Garry Hebb (11)
Firs Primary School

AUTUMN LEAVES

Autumn leaves falling like ballet dancers twirling in the air.
Their rich colours glowing in the darkness as they float to the ground.
Their colours glowing like rubies and diamonds as they get
                                                    trampled on.
The fast movement is like a whirlpool whizzing through the air.
The crunching sound stands out as they wrinkle up.
It's like fireworks exploding into the air as they twirl to the ground.
The stunned people watch as the glittering leaves fall to the ground.

Adam Robson (11)
Firs Primary School

BLUE AND WHITE DAY

Blue and white day
Sparks of sun drifting above your head
Swarms of bees fly carefully around trees
Rain like crystals drifting from the sky
Bluebells chime and dance in a warm shelter
Birds in the swinging trees chirp and sing to people as they pass by
The sun like a bright orange ball in the centre of the sky.

Chandelle Henry (10)
Firs Primary School

AUTUMN LEAVES

Autumn leaves falling like a carpet
of musty reds and orange.
Autumn leaves falling crunch,
crunch when our feet touch the ground.
Autumn leaves falling like a tornado.
Autumn leaves floating like a feather.
Autumn leaves like a cascade of fireworks.

Natalie Bailey (11)
Firs Primary School

BLUE AND WHITE DAY

Blue and white day
Glistening snow drifts to the ground
Excited children run around gliding through the snow
Every step crunches and brings enjoyment
A cool breeze ends the day.

Sarah Jones (10)
Firs Primary School

GOODBYE SUMMER, HELLO AUTUMN

Goodbye summer now you're gone
There'll be no more glimmering sun about
Why can't you stay just another day?
We'll play together under your beautiful sparkle
And at night we'll sleep under the moonlight
The very next day we will get up and play
A bit later on we'll go for a ride
We'll go up to the sky and play with the moon
And when the bell rings for my tea
I'll say goodbye and see you next year
Maybe next year you could stay in my house
We could play games and run about
Goodbye summer see you next year.

Hello autumn and your lovely breeze
Down start the falling of the leaves
In the shades of brown and golden, yellow
When it is dry they crunch and munch
But when it is wet they slip and slide
In our garden the leaves look a mess
They could take all day to clear away.

Katrina Sweetser-Hawkes (10)
Firs Primary School

SUMMER

The summer was here and now it's gone,
the blue sky dies and turns into musty grey.
The cool, white suncream goes away.
The scents drift away to some other place.
No more birds sing, no more gleaming sun
because summer was here and now it's
gone, because autumn fought like a raging
tiger digging its claws into the summer sun.

Sarah Willis (11)
Firs Primary School

AFRICA

The lions look for their prey,
But the zebras run away.
Elephants tramp all day,
And snakes slither away.
Monkeys swing from tree to tree,
Right across the canopy.
Leopards run as fast as they can,
The rainforest covers a big span of Africa.
People are starving from hunger,
They have no water as well.
So let us help Africa to live.

Juan C Herraiz (8)
Greenbank School

AUTUMN

Leaves are falling off the trees,
Golden, crimson, brown and red,
Falling so softly to the ground,
Not a bang, not a clang,
Just crackle, crackle, crackle.

The clock turns back,
Hallowe'en comes along,
With all the ghosts and ghouls,
Apples you pick, plums you eat,
And blackberry pie for a special treat.

Conkers, acorns, hibernation,
Bonfire night, and frosty cars,
All those things happen in
Autumn!

Sophie Whittle (9)
Greenbank School

FIREWORKS

Fireworks explode everywhere,
Bang, crash,
Here comes the banger,
Next is a Catherine wheel,
Round and round it goes,
I would like to light one of those,
Sparklers spell out my name,
This is the rocket out in the sky,
Bang, it's gone up high,
As I eat my toffee apple,
Bright colours in the air everywhere.

Matthew Williamson (8)
Greenbank School

FIREWORK FUN

The bonfire has begun,
We are going to have lots of fun.
Some small faces inside,
Watching the fireworks scream and glide,
One little child shouts *fine!*
Forgetting the fireworks stream and shine,
We have to stay out of the roped ground,
One small child is scared of the sound,
Inside comes more sound from the animals,
The watching area is lighted up with a candle,
Whilst the next firework is planted in some sand,
We are watching the flashing grand,
We all sit down for treacle toffee,
My mum asks anyone for tea or coffee,
We each have a sparkler,
Whilst the adults laugh over coffee and lager,
Now the bonfire is finally over,
Our friends go back to Dover,
I go to bed,
And remember colours blue, green and red.

Jenna Wayne (9)
Greenbank School

PINK

A rose quartz glistening in the setting sun,
Pink roses and tulips swaying in the breeze,
Flamingos sleeping on one leg,
Dirty pigs rolling in mud,
The tips of daisies a beautiful pink,
All blowing in the wind.

Candyfloss fresh from a carnival,
Pink panther prowling around,
Rosy pink cheeks gleaming from the cold,
Strawberry ice-cream deliciously sweet,
Raspberries mashed with cream.

Rachel Sheldon (8)
Greenbank School

AUTUMN LEAVES

Crimson,
Brown,
Gold and hazel,
Orange,
Yellow,
Green.

Crispy,
Curly,
Twisting,
Turning,
Floating,
Falling.

Rustling under your feet,
Flitting away down the street,
Golden carpets made of leaves.

Like a butterfly,
Or landing bird,
Just like a boat on the sea,
Beautiful autumn leaves.

Richard Rawlings (9)
Greenbank School

AUTUMN

Autumn, autumn, beautiful autumn
The leaves fall off in autumn
Twirling, twisting, floating, swaying
The colours are lovely
Bronze, crimson, brown, red and yellow
Falling to the ground softly
The flaming fire on Bonfire night
Hear the fireworks crackle
Conkers shine, conkers may be round
May be bumpy, may be flat
Time goes back one hour
Making the days short and the nights long
Animals hibernating, birds fly south to a warmer place
Trick or treating, Hallowe'en
Eating yummy sweets.

Tim Watkins (8)
Greenbank School

AFRICA

Monkeys, lions, bears and frogs
Where they grow a lot of crops.
Cheetahs, tigers, ants and spiders
And a lot of camel riders.
No food, no grass, nor trees
Isn't there anyone who can help them apart from me?
Poor old Africa, I wish I could help, so help
Help, please help Africa!

Matthew Griffin (8)
Greenbank School

AUTUMN

Leaves falling off the trees
Crackling, floating and twisting
Animals hibernating under the ground
and up high in the trees
Morning frost crackling on my face
Schools have changed from netball to hockey
We wrap up warm when going outside
and curl up by the fire when inside
colours everywhere have changed from green and brown
to red, bronze, crimson and orange
Colours of the rainbow spread over the earth
Beams of light shine on the trees
Sharp old winds help the trees drop their
leaves to make a crimson and bronze
carpet on the floor.

Sophia Copley (9)
Greenbank School

AUTUMN

Leaves are falling - bronze leaves and crimson leaves
Animals are collecting shiny green acorns ready for winter
Children, collecting round, smooth conkers and acorns
The smell of fires as the nights get colder
And the days get shorter and the nights get longer
Sharp silver icicles hanging off the roof.
Fruit is falling off the trees,
Big red and juicy apples are my favourite.
At Bonfire night treacle toffee is on all children's minds
If I look out of the window,
All I can see is a big carpet of golden leaves.

Richard Hodgins (9)
Greenbank School

CHRISTMAS POEM

You can feel the breeze
As Santa flows through the leaves.
He brings all the presents for us
As the reindeers catch flight
Holding on very tight.
As they fly down onto the roof
While their hooves are a clatter,
I run to the window to see what is the matter.
Then a whoosh to the sky where Rudolph will fly,
Away where the polar bears grow.
Santa unloads his sack
And sits down for a snack.
Then snores till the next Christmas snow.

Felicity Rankin (9)
Greenbank School

RED

Red tropical fish swim through the water,
Fires of burning flames,
Rose shiny red,
The sun is rising and setting again,
Rubies are sparkling all day long,
Flags which are red,
Beware,
For the Red Devils will win the European Cup,
Red blood coming out of our skin,
Blood coming in and out of our red hearts,
Cheeks are bright red,
The red apples, hard and round.

Mark Bowen (8)
Greenbank School

WHITE

The blossom is windy white
Curling, whirling in sight
Snow comes every year
And freezes you to a blossom fair
Crystals sparkling in caves
People see them and get amazed
Snowmen are built and melt and come again
Thick clouds come from the sea
And rain heavily on the towns
Polar bears hide themselves
So predators cannot see them lying in the snow
Icebergs big as cathedrals
Like islands touring the world
Ice-creams are white and tasty
And put a smile on your face
Snowdrops are falling, from where?

Adrian Wu (9)
Greenbank School

SILVER

A glistening diamond, a shimmer, a shine
Sun on snow, the colour all mine
Clouds and tips of waves bending and tumbling
The moon in the night sky high and far away
Looks like white but shines like light
Dew on a blade of new green grass
Raindrops in a misty sky
Silver stars glinting in space
Ice on a silver frosty day
These are all the silver things
I can think of today.

Sophie Bryan (8)
Greenbank School

SPACE

Looking up at the shimmering, silver stars,
As if someone had lit a million candles.
But what lies beyond those stars?
I look harder but all I can see is a coat of black,
So I start to imagine.
I pass Saturn, aliens skiing on its rings,
Playing football and lots of other things.
Aliens trying to fly round Jupiter in 80 days.
I visit Pluto, it's very cold like an ice world.
Houses, chairs, tables of ice but the weather is not very nice.
I stop imagining and look up at the stars
And wonder if it's really like that on Saturn, Pluto and Mars.

Emma Dickinson (11)
Greenbank School

DINOSAURS

Monstrous lizards thundering around,
Killing then eating anything they found.
The giant T-Rex that wandered about,
Although big and strong, very dumb.
The Velociraptor stands as high as 10 feet tall,
And is one of the deadliest pack hunters of all.
Although very big is the Brachiosaurus,
It's a simple plant eater unlike others that are smaller.
No matter how fast or strong or tall,
All were killed by a cloud of dust when it blocked out the sun.

Peter Crocker (10)
Greenbank School

CREATURES GREAT AND SMALL

The smooth, spotted cheetah,
Slick and sly,
The one who caught my eye,
Lurks in the grass,
Waiting,
Then leaps for its prey,
As it screams and dies.

The long, green crocodile,
Swims along,
With its eyes afloat,
Gobbles up a fish before you hear the gulp.

The big bald eagle,
Beak so sharp,
Its deafening shriek,
Is heard afar,
Swoops down to catch
A lizard, chick or a rat.

A little mouse scurries by,
To get to his house under the floor,
But the silly old cat,
Does not know that,
The entrance to the hole,
Is under the mat.

Andrew Dickson (10)
Greenbank School

INSECTS OF THE WORLD

Insects are beastly things
Naughty as insects can be
Strong yet ugly they wander in the open air
Even the ants are being naughty to me
Cautiously walking around, watching and listening
for danger is everywhere
Turbulent winds are blowing around so insects cannot fly
Small insects, big insects, they're all the same in some way
Orange, blue or green, insects of all colours
Flies are an annoying insect
They've small wings and a very big buzz
Hundreds of them buzzing around sending people into frustration
Ever so nice, ever so beautiful, the butterflies glide around
With or without grace the beetle is still the best
Other insects are like the beetle but they are special in the world
Rather nice ones, rather not nice ones, but all the same
Looking and sightseeing all insects do for they move about
Dozens of insects all the same, all known to the world

Andrew McGeorge (11)
Greenbank School

FOOTBALL!

Famous grounds we're going to,
Oh! Look they are coming out,
Off they go and they score,
The fans are on their feet to roar,
'Blast!' say the other team,
All the team run to congratulate,
Later on they score again,
Longer than ever the fans now cheer.

Matthew Galloway (10)
Greenbank School

BUTTERFLY HAIKU

Very bright colours,
Bright as flowers in the ground,
They are butterflies.

Butterfly colours,
Blue, white, yellow, red and green,
They're colours I've seen.

Up high in the sky,
The butterflies flutter by,
Softly in the air.

Nicola Bowen (10)
Greenbank School

I'VE DONE SOMETHING WRONG

Oh dear I've done something wrong,
I've gone and ripped his beautiful song.
He tried to hit me in the face,
I told him to get out of this place.
Then I threw him over a hump,
On his knee came a great lump.
I gave him a blow to the head,
Now he is lying in his bed.

Marcus Budgett (10)
Greenbank School

REPTILES

The iguana's scaly skin is as hard as fingernails,
The slippery snake slithers about,
when it strikes it never fails.
The crocodile at the edge of the water
awaits for some fish to slaughter.

Reptiles need to keep warm,
so what they dread is a violent storm.
The reptiles can't get cold or they will
die and be a legend of old.

Andrew Jakubowski (11)
Greenbank School

SATURN

In the darkness, way out in space,
Is the mighty Saturn, swirls of colour on its face.
With its rings of dust and swirling pattern,
The planet with the twelve moons is Saturn.

Sixth in the solar system,
Saturn has its place,
Saturn has its freedom,
It has its own space.

Carla Rankin (11)
Greenbank School

COSMIC

C is for keeping in contact with someone else
O is for the orbit that travels around the earth
S is for the dark and starry night
M is for the bright shining moon
I is for the inner space
C is for the comet that shoots across the sky

S is for the spaceman who goes from planet to planet
T is for the countdown, ten, nine, eight, seven, six
A is for alien who returns into space
R is for the rocket with people on it from the earth

S is for the scary, scary night
P is for when we want to land on a planet
A is for the alien
C is for the captain in charge of the spaceship
E is for the eye that looks at you all night
S is for the spaceship that is flying up high
H is for the hotness from the sun
I is for the icy planets
P is for the planet which is Pluto.

Rebecca Berry (10)
Hurstclough Primary School

COSMIC

C is for cosmic, the name of this theme.
O is for outer space that can only be seen.
S is for the stars so many and so bright.
M is for meteor that races through the night.
I is for inner space where nobody can go.
C is for the comet, let's all have a go.

Kirsty Jordan (9)
Hurstclough Primary School

MY FRIEND STEPHANIE

My friend Stephanie is really kind to me,
She helps me in everything I do.

She laughs like a hyena,
And sings like a cheeping bird,
She walks like a mysterious crawling cat,
And she runs like the howling wind.

Her hair glows like the golden sun,
Her eyes are as blue as a sprinkling waterfall,
Her lips are as red as blood,
And her skin is as soft as fur.

My friend Stephanie is really kind to me,
And she helps me in everything I do.

Ann-Marie Lawrence (11)
Park Road Primary School

CITY LIGHTS

Blurred reflection on the cobbled stone pavement,
Office lights go on as they tower above me,
Car lights glitter as they dance around the dirty city,
The city gains a life of its own as it awakens with light,
The drips of rain that fall from the roofs drop into a colourful pool,
Shop windows dazzle passers by and tempt them to shop . . .
shop . . . shop,
Traffic lights glisten - red, orange, green,
And the dappled light shining through the trees looks like a
broken mirror.

Laura Howe (11)
Park Road Primary School

CITY LIGHTS

The bright glistening city street lamps shimmer with awakening light,
Traffic lights like bright green, red and amber coloured diamonds,
Dazzling as they change colour.

Neon lights gleaming with cascading colours sparkling like a
radiant fire,
Spotlights glow and blink like the eyes of a wide awake owl.

Flickering lights dancing and chasing in the shop window to attract
people's attention,
Beaming headlights of cars reflecting on the dark, filthy, pebbled road.

The city is full of different kinds of glistening lights.

Stephanie Hamer (10)
Park Road Primary School

CITY LIGHTS

Fierce lights pounding out in cascading colours,
Dancing round the city twinkling and sparkling,
Awakening lights flash like a ray beam,
The traffic lights flash red, amber and green,
Lights shimmer astonishingly in pool water,
Car lights shine and reflect from corner to corner,
Restaurant lights flash wickedly to attract attention,
Gleaming colours peak through breezy trees,
Glittering and sparkling colours flash out with joy around the city.

Andrew Colclough (11)
Park Road Primary School

My Mum

Hair as soft
as silk,
brown like mahogany
wood.
Eyes as big as apples,
blue like a tropical sea.
Loving and caring she is
for me,
and for my brother and
sister.
She picks me up when
I am down.
She's always proud
if I try hard.
These things about
her I've come to
adore,
and as you can see
she's the perfect mum
for me.

Hayley Fallon (10)
Park Road Primary School

Seasons

Buds turn to blossom, pink and white,
The sun now shines and fills the land with light.
Sheep give birth, and the lambs learn to leap,
The yellow, diminutive chicks chirped their first cheep.

The blazing, hot, sweltering sun awakes,
The excitement shows on our faces about our long summer breaks.
Aeroplanes flying, boats sailing, trains full,
Not a day without a pleasure, nor a day which is dull.

Autumn arrives ever so quick,
Conkers so shiny, never knowing which to pick.
A magic spell of colours is set alight,
Royal red, flaky gold, illuminous yellow, exploding orange,
all so bright.

The cold shivering branches bare, with not a leaf in sight,
The howls so fierce it seems to bite.
Winter has arrived, the gloomy, dull moon starts to sneer,
Laughing at our frozen earth, as the mysterious stars appear.

Justine Woolley (9)
Park Road Primary School

IF I COULD WIN THE LOTTERY . . .

If I could win the lottery,
I'd become a millionaire.
I would sack 1000 companies,
And unpollute the air.

If I could win the lottery,
I'd tell the wars to end,
I'd teach the world to sing,
Even though it would send me round the bend.

If I could win the lottery,
I'd wake myself from slumber,
And every time I'd fall asleep,
I'd just begin to wonder.

Nadine Martyniuk (11)
Park Road Primary School

BONFIRE NIGHT

The sky was dark and smoky.
I could hear the crackling of the roaring, glittering red fire.
Sparks flew up into the air.
The sound of people talking was deafening to my ears.
Unexpectedly there was a *whiz, pop!* And down came a cascade
of colours.
Then I came into reach of the toxic smell of the crackling fire.
The screamers sounded like millions of children all screaming together.
Bonfire night makes me think of Parkin, as crunchy as crisps,
and treacle toffee all slimy, yum!

Carolyn Fletcher (10)
Park Road Primary School

BEAU

Eyes of a chocolate lover,
Got separated from his mother.
Fur as white as snow,
His name is pronounced 'Bow'.
Tail curled up like a shell,
He barks when he hears a bell.
Eyes like alert radar,
Try to get jam jars.
Bark of the werewolf in a tale,
When he goes near people they go pale.
Paws as puffed up as a hedgehog,
Oh yeah, he's a dog.

Ryan Parker (11)
Park Road Primary School

SQUIRRELS

Squirrels are cute,
Strange and funny.
Jumping from tree to tree,
How can they do it? How can it be?

With hand-like paws,
And sharp clinging claws,
All colours, red, brown and grey,
Coming out in April, June and May.

Forging for nuts and acorns too,
To see them through the winter,
And cold, harsh nights.

Charlotte Yeoman (9)
Park Road Primary School

FOOTBALL

Screaming, shouting,
Cheers aloud,
Football songs sung by the crowd.

Balls flying all around,
The ref's whistle blows,
A free kick given,
The crowd arises,
The player runs to strike the ball,
Goal! It is tied 1-1 all.

Alex Jones (11)
Park Road Primary School

My Pet

Eyes as red as a burning flame,
But full of warmth and love for me.
Her ears prick up every time I call her by name,
And purrs so soft and sweet.
Her fur is as black as the midnight sky,
With white patches like the glowing midnight moon.
She's always ready and eager to play,
And when she does, it's affection that fills her eyes.
I see in her a majestic creature,
Who will be in my heart forever,
Even when she leaves this life
And goes onto a perfect place,
Where only peace and love fills the air.

Rachel Cahill (11)
Park Road Primary School

City Lights

The city awakens with beams of light,
The neon lights hang on the shop wall,
Cascading with colours as they flash,
The bright, piercing lights cling onto the corner shop attracting you
towards them just like a magnet.
The street lamp just like a nocturnal animal's eyes staring down
on the bare, dry, cobbled pavement leaving a glowing, orange pool,
bringing the ground to life.
The traffic lights blink from colour to colour,
The car headlights dance around the city bringing excitement
to the night.

Lynsey Wright (9)
Park Road Primary School

THE ALIEN'S TRIP

In a bright red rocket
An alien started his trip
He had lots of food and water
But he was worried he might get space sick.

He took off from his planet
Called planet Colerite
And when he saw Jupiter
He thought what a wonderful sight.

Then he landed on Saturn
And ran right round the rings
Then he set off back to Colerite
To tell them of some wonderful things.

Nicola Camm (11)
Prospect Vale Primary School

STARS

Stars are shining in the sky
while you and me are floating by.
We look around and see
all the children happy and glee.
Stars are twinkling ever so bright
in the darkness of the night.

Rebecca Winder (10)
Prospect Vale Primary School

JIMMY RON

I knew a man called Jimmy Ron
Who thought he was better than everyone
Then one day he had an idea
That he would use a gardening shear
He thought that he would fly through space
And have a go at a shooting star race
He was at the starting line ready to go . . .
When 3, 2, 1, he banged his toe
But he still wanted to go
His head must have been mashed
He was all on his way
Oh no, he crashed.

Faye Daniels (11)
Prospect Vale Primary School

SPRING

Spring is the time the sweet birds sing,
watch out for the buzzing bees that sting.
Look for the kittens,
they'll be playing with their mittens.
Watch the lambs learn to play,
jumping around in the hay.
At the end of the day
we will say have a happy Easter holiday.

Katie Doughty (10)
Prospect Vale Primary School

MY TRIP IN SPACE

Gliding past the Milky Way,
the sun, the moon, the stars,
and whizzing past planets like
Saturn, Pluto and Mars.

Landing on the moon
was really lots of fun,
placing my flag in the middle,
being aware of the red hot sun.

But soon it was all over,
my journey back to Earth began,
but of course I will remember,
what a lucky girl I am.

Laura Dorsett (10)
Prospect Vale Primary School

EASTER EGGS

Easter eggs are very good,
they're yummy, funny and
they're good for your tummy.
Some are big, some are small,
the rest are very tall.
Some are ugly, some are nice
but one thing they're not the same price.

Shuhaib Shaffi (11)
Prospect Vale Primary School

FRIENDSHIP

Caring for your friend,
And being polite,
That's what friendship,
Is all about.
You should respect your friends,
For what they are,
And never ask,
For a chocolate bar.
Never be cheeky,
Always be nice,
Before you open your mouth,
Think twice.
Never be bad,
Always be good,
Treat your friends,
The way you should.

Sarah Marchant (11)
Prospect Vale Primary School

COSMIC

As I set off and go to bed
I see space hiding around in my head
I dream all about the moon in the sky
And I see comets floating by
I dream of the black hole whirling around
As I get hotter I start to make a sound
My body feels weightless
As I become very dreamless.

Anthony Dando (10)
Ridge Hill Primary School

MIRACLE BIRD

I'm flying through space
On a miracle bird
Its silver wings glitter and glow
As we pass through the stars
Which light the dark sky
My fingertips glow as the silver reflects
From the shooting star that passes
As we whiz through
Space itself
The coldness pricks my cheeks
And makes them icy blue
My hair flows behind me
Like a golden cloak.

Claire Walton (11)
Ridge Hill Primary School

COSMIC

If I was an astronaut,
I'd zoom far into deep black space,
Watching the hot swirling asteroids and the lonely satellites.
The dark atmospheric layer and shining black holes,
I'd see the big calm planets in a peaceful wave,
The sun would be my light, my soul and my life,
It is a whizzing place especially for me!

Samantha Lee (11)
Ridge Hill Primary School

COSMIC!

The things I see up here
in the sky.
Planets, asteroids whizzing by.
When the night falls I start to dazzle.
Quiet and far away I bring
the light with all my mates
into the dark night.
Sometimes I see a few rockets
and planes flying past.
And I'd love to travel that fast.
Aliens from Jupiter are the best
but if they're from Mars or
Saturn, then watch your *step!*

Sophie Booth (10)
Ridge Hill Primary School

SIGHTS IN SPACE

I wish I was in a spaceship
Whizzing everywhere
Dazzled by the light
Floating in the air
See the planets whirling
Comets zooming too
I'd watch the stars go rushing by
And the big white moon in the big black sky.

Richard Flanagan (11)
Ridge Hill Primary School

SPACE ENVIRONMENT

Space flowers are six feet tall,
They have marble stems of red and gold,
Their huge leaves are the shape of a perfect star,
Their swirly petals match the stems,
But these are silver and blue,
The pollen inside is golden dust,
What a shame the aliens picked them all.

Space trees are microscopic,
You cannot see them at all,
Their thin trunks are made of silver,
Their leaves are of solid gold,
What a shame the aliens squashed them.

Space grass is three feet high,
When you touch its sharp blades a sensation overcomes you,
Its texture is as rough as sandpaper,
Even though it's pure silk.
What a shame the aliens ate it all.

Olivia Burgess (11)
Ridge Hill Primary School

SPACE

From the moon the earth looks like a marble
With twisting and swirling greens and blues
Murky clouds that look like marshmallows
And all other planets gleaming around!
The sun is its best friend.
The earth is twirling forever,
I don't think it will ever stop.

Tanya Murphy (11)
Ridge Hill Primary School

THE ALIEN

It was whirling round my garden like a shiny starfish,
It looked like it was waiting for someone or something
I felt like I had the biggest gobstopper in the world in my mouth,
The spaceship sounded like a washing machine.
It landed with a thud, and with a clash the alien popped out,
Landing with a bang on the floor
Like a blob of jelly wobbling towards me
So I hid behind my dustbin, watching it wobble along
With excitement.
As it was getting closer I was reversing back,
Until I could go no further
I had no choice,
I had to crawl out from behind my bin.
I walked towards it shaking
It scuttled into its spaceship and flew off
Never to be seen again.

Emma Hogg (10)
Ridge Hill Primary School

SPACE

A huge black velvet cushion,
with sewn on little pearls.
A large embroidered ball of fire,
and a small white golf ball moon.
Mars is a fierce red bull's eye,
Saturn is a round pebble with a lot of ripples,
Uranus is a medium sized green apple,
Venus is a golden plum,
Pluto is a playful black ping pong ball,
And Earth is a mixture of all.

Sarah Chatterton (11)
Ridge Hill Primary School

STARS

It's a diamond in the sky,
Hanging up there like a puppet on a string,
There are so many up there,
You can't even count them,
When I feel all uptight,
I lie upon the grass at night, staring,
Me and them, white dots,
We stare at each other, all night,
Then they start to fade in the dawning light,
I feel the sadness leave me,
A peace descends,
And another night is gone.

Daniel Forrester (10)
Ridge Hill Primary School

SPACESHIP

There I was scared and cold,
A big silver ball let down a ladder
As it came close I felt a lot sadder,
A tear dropped down
Like a rippling raindrop,
Then it landed
I found I was stranded
In a big green field
Into the air I spun up above
And in the dark night sky
I was not cold nor scared anymore.

Jaya Patel (10)
Ridge Hill Primary School

UNTITLED

In my garden,
Looking up,
I saw a spinning top in the air,
Red flashing lights like a fairground.
Slowly, slowly it came down,
Landed on the green, wavy grass.
As it landed I backed away.
The door opened,
Whoosh!
Slowly, fearfully I crept forward,
A blob of slime plopped out.
I felt terrified as he shivered towards me,
The hairs stuck up on the back of my head,
Nearer,
Nearer,
Nearer,
And then
Gloop!

Gareth Culpin (10)
Ridge Hill Primary School

STARS

The stars came out
I was happy again
I sat on the grass just watching them
But shortly after, they faded away like a mist
The day began
I was sad again until the stars came out
Another night
When they came out
I started to watch like I was hypnotised.

Daryl Cornthwaite (10)
Ridge Hill Primary School

THE DAY THE EARTH DIED

It came floating down like snowflakes,
Its bright orange lights floating round it,
Silent like someone had turned the
volume down on it.
In a cloud of smoke the door opened,
Out crawled a blob shaking like jelly,
At its side it held a gun,
It began,
Destruction!
Everything in sight,
The earth was burnt to a cinder,
Nothing was left standing.

Christopher Alexander (10)
Ridge Hill Primary School

SPACE

It's a dark satin sheet with tiny diamonds shining in the light
with a small blue creature floating like a feather.
I look through its eyes into the darkness,
to see all the colourful planets
twirling around like a basketball on a finger.
Enjoyment floods through me like warm water running
down my body.
I have a souvenir in my mind to remind me of the
wonderful time.

Stacey Healey (10)
Ridge Hill Primary School

COSMIC

There is a man,
On our road called Dan,
Who wanted to fly to Saturn,
But yet he did not know,
That the creatures there speak Latin,

When he got there and found that out,
He just ranted and raved about,
Because of this he decided to go to Pluto.
On his way,
He decided to go home and play Ludo.

Leanne Waddock (10)
Ridge Hill Primary School

COSMIC

Up, up in the sky,
Spaceships can fly
Well zoom to the moon
Space, space is a wonderful place.

Spinning around as fast as a ball,
All of a sudden I see something tall,
Oh no . . . it's a UFO with one big toe.

Kayleigh Morris (11)
Ridge Hill Primary School

SPACE

Faster and faster into the night,
Galaxy glows so big and bright,
Mars is alight all night,
Flying through the sky as fast as can be,
All of a sudden space sees me.

Rachel Heap (10)
Ridge Hill Primary School

WORLD WAR TWO

Children getting on the train,
Saying bye to their dads.
Dads going off to fight.
The siren's going off,
They get in their shelters.
They hear bang, bang,
The bombs go off.
People saying
'I hope the next bomb does not land here.'
People running and screaming 'Help.'
People getting killed
The next siren goes off
We come out and see fire everywhere.

Ashley Parker (11)
St Basil's RC Primary School, Widnes

OUT OF THIS WORLD

A soaring star,
A land from afar,
You find them in space,
But you have to wear a mask over your face,
You will find nine large things,
Some of them have rings,
Planets are what they are,
The sun is only a giant star,
Planets are cool,
You learn about them in school,
They're shaped like a ball,
And their moons are so small,
There are nine planets, don't argue with that,
If they could roll they'd knock you flat!

Katie Hodgson (10)
St Basil's RC Primary School, Widnes

WORLD WAR TWO

At war people are fighting
At home people are cooking

At war people are dying
At home people are cleaning

At war people are scared
At home people are sewing

At war people are hiding
At home people are worrying

When will the war end?

Samantha Pye (10)
St Basil's RC Primary School, Widnes

THE LAST DAY OF TERM

The last day of term
is my favourite kind of day
we scream and shout and laugh and play
then we throw our work away.

The last day of term is really cool
because it's the last day of school
I don't like school any other day
that's when the teachers get in your way.

The last day of term
I just can't stay
because I want to go home and play
I like to play with the boys
then I play with the toys.

Alan Hyland (10)
St Basil's RC Primary School, Widnes

WAR TIME

At war people are fighting,
At home people are scared,
Please stop the war.
At war people are dying,
At home people are crying,
Please stop the war.
At war nurses are caring,
At home people are cooking,
Please stop the war.
At war people are gunning,
At home people are running,
Please stop the war.

Robert Rolt (10)
St Basil's RC Primary School, Widnes

WHY WON'T THE WAR STOP?

At home women are mending,
While the men are at war.
Why won't the war stop?

At home women are cleaning,
While the men are struggling.
Why won't the war stop?

The women are worrying,
In case the men get hurt.
Why won't the war stop?

At home people are crying,
In case someone dies.
Why won't the war stop?

At home people are crying,
While the men are fighting.
Why won't the war stop?

Samantha Knight (10)
St Basil's RC Primary School, Widnes

FUZZY ELECTRICITY

E lectric flows through the fuzzy air
L iving deeply in the pylons
E verlasting electric in our homes
C overing millions of houses
T ripping over clouds
R oaring lightning over the lands
I   live along the thin wires
C onducting electricity is fun.

Laura Pitt (9)
St Basil's RC Primary School, Widnes

SOUNDS

Round our school we heard
Chris Vobe banging across the hall
The cars speeding away
Our papers whispering in the wind.

Round our school we heard
Miss Murray talking loud and clear
Cups clanking in the kitchen
Radiators clicking and blowing in our faces

Round our school we heard
Miss Harrison shouting
Crisps rattling away
Coat hangers banging together in my ear
And out the other.

Debbie Carmon (9)
St Basil's RC Primary School, Widnes

THE STORM

Calm skies, seas too,
Heavy clouds, crashing sea
Lightning flashing, blinding,
Banging, howling thunder
Thrown over deck,
Raging fierce wind
Waves tumble,
Ship crumbles
Slippery slidy decks,
Yelling a lot loudly
Ship breaks
Calm again.

Ashleigh Pierce (8)
St Basil's RC Primary School, Widnes

FRIDAY THE 13TH

Woke up fell out of bed
pulling down the wallpaper
Mum screaming and shouting at me
I might have known it's
      Friday the 13th.

Falling down the stairs
get to the bottom
I think I've broken my neck
good grief I haven't
I might have known it's
      Friday the 13th.

Playing a game of tick.
Oh no what's happening?
Skidding, sliding everywhere
I get control of my feet
a tap on the shoulder
who's there?
I try to turn round
I might have known it's
      Friday the 13th.

Elizabeth Allen (8)
St Basil's RC Primary School, Widnes

FRIDAY THE 13TH

Oh no it is Friday the 13th,
And I've got the chickenpox,
I am not going to school,
Everything will go wrong,
Oh no it's Friday the 13th!

My school is haunted,
The floors are creaking,
Doors are slamming behind me,
Oh no it's Friday the 13th.

I must have got out of bed the wrong side,
I feel something on my shoulder,
There is someone standing behind me,
This is a very creepy day,
Because it's Friday the 13th!

I go outside to play,
I start running,
And I slip on ice,
Someone picks me up,
And takes me into a dark room,
Oh no it's Friday the 13th!

Hannah Edwards (8)
St Basil's RC Primary School, Widnes

I AM A FIREWORK

As I get picked out of the box
I'm trying not to be scared.
Everyone shouts and cheers as I am
The biggest one of all.
I get stuck into the pole in the ground.
I'm starting to get scared now.
He strikes the match and lights the fuse.
I'm nearly on fire.
'Boom' I shoot up into the air
And burst out into beautiful flames
I know I am going to hit the ground
Trembling with my fear
As I hear everyone clapping and cheering
And see everyone in amazement looking at me
As now I am going to hit, fade out and cry
I hit the ground, I shout
'Goodbye.'

Samantha King (11)
St Basil's RC Primary School, Widnes

AROUND OUR SCHOOL WE HEARD . . .

Loud footsteps running across the hall
Children working, teachers bawling
Clanging, slamming, banging doors
Pencils sliding across the page

Around our school we heard . . .
Chairs banging, clanging together
Mrs Tracey typing on the computer
With her noisy fingers

Mrs Harrison shouting, with a fierce loud voice
Mrs Essary talking noisily to the children
Mr Anker cutting wood with a sharp, loud
Dangerous saw

Children banging, smashing chairs against
The table, shouting with their loud mouths

I just wish it was quiet!

Naomi Anderson (8)
St Basil's RC Primary School, Widnes

OUTSIDE OUR SCHOOL

Outside our school
We can hear
People shouting
Dogs barking
Cars rushing

Outside our school
We can hear
Horses galloping
Trees rustling
Birds singing

Outside our school
We can hear
Doors slamming
Visitors laughing
Children talking

And that is what we could hear.

Sally Colligan (9)
St Basil's RC Primary School, Widnes

FRIDAY 13TH

I'm sitting upstairs
My chair starts to spin
I must have known
It's Friday 13th.

Everything is still
I'm starting to get a chill
I must have known
It's Friday 13th.

What's gone wrong?
No breath of wind
I must have known
It's Friday 13th.

It's really scary
Or is that just Mel B?
I must have known
It's Friday 13th.

I look outside
My finger turns to ice
I must have known
It's Friday 13th.

I turn the clock back
But here it comes again
What a Friday!

Anthony Gee (8)
St Basil's RC Primary School, Widnes

LIMERICKS

There was once a rabbit called Fluffy
He went in a room that was stuffy,
He opened a window and shouted hello,
And that was the end of poor Fluffy.

There was once a man from Greece
Who had a poor little niece,
She sat on a swing
And sang diddly ding,
Then found a 5p piece.

There was a girl called Gill,
Who loved to ride down a hill,
She went to a shop
To buy a pork chop,
And that was the girl called Gill.

Tania Walker (8)
St Basil's RC Primary School, Widnes

AROUND OUR SCHOOL WE HEARD

Crashing rulers banging together
Heater roaring and clicking away
Quiet tiptoes across the hall
Laser printer buzzing away
Whistling cars go flying past
Birds cluttering around in the sky
The water bubbling furiously
Banging creaking doors
Crash shut!
Diggers scoop fiercely
Tossing the soil into the air.

Jonathan Floyd (9)
St Basil's RC Primary School, Widnes

AROUND OUR SCHOOL WE HEARD...

Around our school we heard . . .
The engines of the noisy cars
As they pass the metal bars.

Around our school we heard . . .
Dogs barking
And puppies howling.

Around our school we heard . . .
Litter blowing
Where on earth is it going?

Around our school we heard . . .
Teachers in the classroom
Knock, knock, knocking on the door.

Around our school we heard . . .
Running
And people like little birds.

Around our school we heard . . .
Doors slamming
And other doors banging.

Around our school we heard . . .
The water bubbling
Bubbles doubling.

Around our school we heard . . .
Locks buzzing
And Luke being stubborn.

Around our school we heard . . .
Pens and pencils writing
The scratching feels like biting.

Around our school we heard . . .
Mrs Tracey talking
And coat hangers crashing.

What a noisy place this school is!
Crash! Bang! Thump!

Christopher Vobe (8)
St Basil's RC Primary School, Widnes

FRIDAY 13TH

Walking to school
Looking all around me
Bump
I bumped into a lamp post
I might have known
It's Friday the 13th!

Standing in the line
Next minute I slip on some ice
And bump into Laura
I might have known
It's Friday the 13th!

Gazing out of the window
Somebody's tapping me on the shoulder
I turn around
Nobody's there
I might have known
It's Friday the 13th!

Laura Filkins (9)
St Basil's RC Primary School, Widnes

FRIDAY THE 13TH

There's something behind me,
Running across the yard,
Turn around, nothing there,
Oh no it's Friday the 13th!

Rattling closet,
'Hello, anybody there?'
Spooky coat hanger!
Oh no it's Friday the 13th!

Big fat beetle,
'You dare bite me!'
Little scary archway,
Oh no it's Friday the 13th!

Luke Hughes (8)
St Basil's RC Primary School, Widnes

APPLES EATEN ALIVE

I woke up one morning,
I was being eaten alive,
I was lashed and smashed,
I was put in the oven,
I put on my sunglasses,
But I got taken out.

I didn't know what I was going to be,
I felt melted like slime,
I looked above me,
I saw small breadcrumbs all around me,
I was put on a plate, spooned up and eaten alive.
        Arrrgh!

Daniel Jones (9)
St Basil's RC Primary School, Widnes

IT'S NOT FAIR

It's not fair
Why don't they care!
That wasn't a reason to ground me
Just because I jumped in the mud
And slurped in it
And slipped in it
And slapped through the ground!
It took all afternoon
Until I heard a sound
         Oh! No!
It's my dad
'Melissa, Melissa
You've been bad!'

Melissa Pugh (8)
St Basil's RC Primary School, Widnes

THE STORM

The howling wind,
Lashing rain,
Black clouds,
Crashing, lashing water against the boat,
Hanging over the edge of the boat,
Falling and tumbling with barrels,
Crashing against the side of the boat,
Raging storms break the boat,
Boat sinks,
All quiet again!

Christopher McCormick (8)
St Basil's RC Primary School, Widnes

HOMEWORK

1st week

Sir, it's about my homework
The baby ripped it all up Sir
I tried to Sellotape it back up
But it kept falling apart
I tried to glue it
But it kept moving

2nd week

Sir it's about my homework
My brother threw it in the bath Sir
I tried to blow dry it
But the pages went crinkly
So I put baby lotion on it
But it went all soggy

3rd week

Sir it's about my homework
My pencil broke
And I haven't got another one at home
So I couldn't do it

4th week

Sir it's about my homework
The baby didn't rip it up,
My brother didn't throw it in the bath,
And my pencil didn't break
I just didn't do it!

Katie Lyons (8)
St Basil's RC Primary School, Widnes

THE AWFUL HOUSE

Playing on my computer game
Getting better it's good!
My mum shouts me down for tea
I don't know whether I should
Oh it's not fair
Oh they don't understand!

I lie in bed reading away
Suddenly my dad comes in
And says
'Let's call it a day'
Oh it's not fair
Oh they don't understand!

Try to sneak away with my brother's ball
He says 'Hey'
I star to bawl
Oh it's not fair
Oh they don't understand!

My sisters have blisters
They order me about
I start to cry
Like a water spout
Oh it's not fair
Oh they don't understand!

David Prescott (9)
St Basil's RC Primary School, Widnes

'

NOISES

In our school we heard -
Chris' soft light footsteps
Nearly deafened by laughter

Heaters beating out hot air all day
Making classrooms warm every day

In our school we heard -
Doors slamming and chairs clanging
Mrs Turner shouting, paper turning

Pencils scraping against paper
Like nails on a blackboard

The laser printer whirring
Mrs Tracey typing

In our school there are lots of noises!

Simon Smith (9)
St Basil's RC Primary School, Widnes

WORLD WAR TWO

The bombs fall,
They destroy buildings and all
Children and adults die.
They all die but nobody knows why.

Men are called away,
They just have to leave one day.
Food is rationed like eggs and milk,
Clothes are rationed like nylon and silk.

Men are sent away to fly planes,
While women sleep in shelters,
Where once they waited for trains.
All the streets are black,
The bombs hit the floor, *crack, smack!*

The evacuees have a tag with their name on it,
In the train not sure if they are going to be hit.
People are dead.
On the radio 'It will soon be over'
Winston Churchill said.

Martin O'Neill (11)
St Basil's RC Primary School, Widnes

THE STORM

As the peaceful day begins with the sun being born,
A ship sails to this mystical island.
Little do they know what lies ahead.

As the sky turns black,
The wind begins to rage.
The sea bellows and howls
With screams of haunting spirits.
The lightning strikes, lashing out,
As fast as a speeding bullet.

As the sky clears
The sea seems calm
The wind turns to a breeze.
As Mother Nature returns
She brings with her peace and harmony.

Christopher Roberts (9)
St Basil's RC Primary School, Widnes

A HARD LIFE

I was hanging from a tree,
Big and juicy and bright green.
Suddenly I started to slip,
I looked up to the tree,
And a twig fell down and
Bang, bash, crash!

When I woke up I was
In a human house,
I looked around
There was nobody in sight,
I turned around and saw
A banana ask an orange for a fight.
Before I knew it
I was in the bowl
With those two silly, quarrelling fruits.

Then I was picked up,
I thought 'I will be leaving,'
But I was put in a freezer,
And boy was I freezing!
I was in there for two days,
I banged my head,
Am I alive or am I dead.

Andrew Barlow (9)
St Basil's RC Primary School, Widnes

LAST DAY OF TERM

Last day of term
It's really cool

Last day of term
We get out of school

Last day of term
We bring our toys

Last day of term
We make loads of noise

Last day of term
We wear our own clothes

Last day of term
We turn up the music, loads

Last day of term
We go away

Last day of term
All we do is play!

Natalie McCool (9)
St Basil's RC Primary School, Widnes

WAR TIME

Hiding away,
Sirens all day,
Trembling with fear,
With my daughter near.

Hiding away,
Night and day,
Trembling with fear,
The Germans are here.

Hiding away,
As long as I can stay,
Trembling with fear,
The bombs sound so clear.

Katie McKeown (10)
St Basil's RC Primary School, Widnes

THE ALLIGATOR

The alligator is like a radiator,
cold blooded, but when the sun heats him up
he's like a roasted chicken!
Start a fight, he'll give you a good licking.
Teeth that seem to smile at you, he sleeps in
the Nile waiting for a meal or even a deal.
Rip your arm off, he will use the tip to scratch his back
because he lacks energy.
So when you're on the Nile beware,
alligators are there!

Adam Woodward (11)
St Clement's RC Primary School, Runcorn

THE WITCH

Nasty witch, big bad witch.
She's smelly, she stinks,
with a big nose and
horrible toes.
Warts everywhere,
I wouldn't dare mess
with the witch.
I've seen ugly but not as
ugly as the witch.
She cackles at night and gives
me a fright.
She boils children and bats
and bugs.
Hallowe'en is her favourite night,
to scare those trick or treaters
out of sight.

Elizabeth Burquest (10)
St Clement's RC Primary School, Runcorn

CRAZY

I'm as crazy as a bat wearing a hat,
A kangaroo on the loo,
A hippo making stew.

A hen writing with a pen,
A gnat chasing a cat,
A pig in a dinosaur dig.

A crocodile gluing in a file,
A lizard faster than a blizzard,
A mole shovelling coal.

Steven Johnston (10)
St Clement's RC Primary School, Runcorn

SPRING!

Spring is very sensational,
lots of baby animals.
From ewes grow lots of fluffy lambs
and hens grow lots of cute chicks.

It rains like bullets shooting from the sky
which makes flowers grow
with a bit of warm sun
and cows grow lots of calves.

Hens teach their chicks to cackle like proper mothers.
Cows teach their calves to moo like trumpets.
Sheep teach their lambs like old ewes
as spring begins to end.

James Marnell (8)
St Clement's RC Primary School, Runcorn

SPRING

Spring is in the air
And the daffodils grow everywhere.
The lambs have white fluffy coats,
And bounce around.

The beautiful birds fly back home,
To make their nests, tweeting and calling to each other.
In the early sun
The birds sound excited and are having fun.

Sean Bahan (8)
St Clement's RC Primary School, Runcorn

SPRING!

Spring is an Easter season.
Everyone has Easter eggs with shiny paper on them.
They taste yummy!
Animals being born, baby chicks, baby lambs are all very cute.
I like the daffodils blowing in the wind.
Tulips are my favourite flowers.
The sun is so bright in the blue sky and
The clouds are like white bubbles.

Craig Foulkes (7)
St Clement's RC Primary School, Runcorn

SPRING!

In the spring it is the best time of year.
The grass twinkles like stars.
The lambs are like big balls of snow.
The chicks are like daffodil tops.
The goats are like soil on the ground.
The tulips look like red lips.
Crocuses look like elves' hats.
Daffodil tops are like suns.
Quite often it's raining and sometimes sunny.

Joseph Doyle (7)
St Clement's RC Primary School, Runcorn

SPRING!

The daffodils in the spring,
The daffodils in the freezing cold,
They are growing so excellent,
They are like the sun but brighter.
The animals are having babies,
Like cows, chickens and sheep.
The farmers are having a great time,
So you should too because the animals are having babies.
The plants are growing now you must be glad,
It is time for you to go,
So spring is here.

Jemma Haddock (7)
St Clement's RC Primary School, Runcorn

SPRING!

In spring it's the best season.
It is when the leaves come back on the trees.
The leaves look like green ovals.
Baby chicks are born.
The chicks look like fluffy balls.
Calves are born as well, the calves look like they have a beard
When they have taken their milk.

Michael Griffiths (7)
St Clement's RC Primary School, Runcorn

SPRING!

Daffodils and tulips all around the place,
all different flowers you can name except a few.
Baby lambs are born and chicks as well,
maybe you can see one by a well.

The trees grow buds and the bushes grow
leaves that look like green blobs of rain.
The air has a funny smell of fresh clothes
coming out of a washing machine.
The flowers come from a tiny seed
that grows into a beautiful crocus.

The sheep run about in the lovely air around them.
The chicks learn how to quack properly.
The grass sparkles and glitters too,
it's a shiny green colour,
I can remember what it looks like.
The sun shines and makes a reflection,
I love the sun.

Erin Smith (7)
St Clement's RC Primary School, Runcorn

BORED

Bored is the colour brown.
Bored tastes like a rotten egg.
Bored smells like a burning rubber.
Bored looks like a big fire.
Bored is not very good
Because you can't do anything.

Gary Bennett (10)
St Clement's RC Primary School, Runcorn

SPRING!

The spring is beautiful
and the flowers are like lollipops
flowing in the breeze.
My favourite flowers are tulips
just like the colour on my lips.

There are lots of flowers to see,
trumpet daffodils and cute little daisies.
The sun blazes through a glass window.
I love baby animals like lambs and foals.

I like the spring, the spring likes me.
Spring is so tender, I love it so much,
like the boats on the sea.
The flowers are so beautiful,
I can just imagine.

Hayley Meagher (7)
St Clement's RC Primary School, Runcorn

SPRING!

Spring can be a wondrous thing.
Just as spectacular as a bird's wing.
It might rain but it doesn't cause any pain.
Spring makes me sing.
In the winter the birds fly away
but then they come back to stay.
In the winter the flowers die away
and I give a little sigh
but then spring comes and I fill with joy.

Rebecca Sargeant (8)
St Clement's RC Primary School, Runcorn

SPRING!

In the spring all the birds come out and
build their nests high in the lollipop trees.

In the spring the chicks and lambs are born.
Every year I see more of them,
see them stroll along the field.
The lambs look like snowflakes
have zoomed from the sky.

The chicks look like the amazing
sun has shone on them.

In the spring the buds come out
looking like large snowdrops.

When it is cold see the candyfloss snow
so small and soft.
The candyfloss looks so sparkly
that I wish I could have some.

I wish it was spring every day.

Alexandra Parkinson (8)
St Clement's RC Primary School, Runcorn

SPRING!

Cold and frosty spring has come.
Daffodils swaying in the breeze.
Lambs are sleeping in the sun.
Birds are tweeting in the sky.
Chicks being born in the blazing sun.
Spring is fun, airy days making the tulips grow.
Spring! Spring! Please don't go.
Spring is the time when animals are born.

Fern Smith (7)
St Clement's RC Primary School, Runcorn

INSIDE THE BOX . . .

Inside the box you will find,
A little mouse that's sweet and kind,
A slithery snake that likes to grind,
Or a daft old bat that's completely blind!

Inside the box you will find,
A borrower that likes to dance,
A six-legged spider that deserves a chance,
Or a little rat that wants a glance.

Inside the box you will find,
A sporty hedgehog that likes to jog,
A pidgy little wishing log,
Or a cat that wants to be a dog.

Rachel Pitt (10)
St Clement's RC Primary School, Runcorn

FEELINGS

Happy.
Happy is yellow.
It tastes like sweets.
It smells like the park with a big slide.
It sounds like a bird singing.
It feels like a puppy licking your hand.

Sad.
Sad is blue.
It smells like the sewers.
It looks like a rain cloud overhead.
It sounds like someone crying.
It feels like gunge.

Sam Allen (10)
St Clement's RC Primary School, Runcorn

FEELINGS

Angry
Is a bright red colour with some yellow and orange in it.

Angry
Tastes like a bitter lemon melting in your mouth
with hot sauce and mustard mixed together.

Angry
Smell like a red-hot volcano
with hot dogs cooking on a barbecue.

Angry
Looks like an earthquake with hot mud
running over you like a tidal wave.

Angry
Sounds like standing on a cat's tail.

Angry
Feels like a rumble in your tummy.

Hannah Pauline (9)
St Clement's RC Primary School, Runcorn

SPRING!

The cold rain dropping down and all snowdrops coming down,
It looks so beautiful.
A lot of daffodils up,
The tulips coming up with the rain coming down every day.
The birds making nests.
The sky dried up like stone.
The chicks with no skin, they look like strawberries in the breeze.
Green grass getting picked.
Lambs getting their tails cut off.

Elizabeth Richardson (8)
St Clement's RC Primary School, Runcorn

FEELINGS

Angry is red.
It tastes like hot peppers.
It smells like burning coal.
It looks like a burning fire.
It sounds like a rumbling volcano.
It feels like I'm on fire.

Happy is yellow.
It tastes like chocolate cake.
It smells like a flower.
It looks like the burning sun.
It sounds like someone laughing.
It feels like a smooth cloth.

Mark McGrath (9)
St Clement's RC Primary School, Runcorn

ANGRY, BORED

Angry is the colour red like fire blazing.
It tastes like spicy chicken with chilli.
It smells like burning rubber just lit.
It sounds like a rumbling volcano.
It feels like a very hot pipe in the sun.

Bored is the colour grey.
It tastes like milk gone off.
It smells like rotten fish.
It sounds like someone humming.
It feels like a leaf.

Bradley Siner (10)
St Clement's RC Primary School, Runcorn

SPRING!

Thank you God for the lovely flowers in the world.
The lovely daffodils because they are so bright, cheerful
and golden in the middle.

I like it when it is raining because it taps on the floor
and it helps the plants to grow.

I like the leaves because they are a lovely colour
and a lovely shape and they look nice.

I love this country because it is so colourful
and there are lovely flowers.

Laura Dixon (8)
St Clement's RC Primary School, Runcorn

FEELINGS

Angry is red.
It tastes like really hot chilli.
It smells like fire smoke flying in the sky.
It looks like rumbling lava.
It sounds like a hurricane.
It feels like fire burning.

Happy is pink.
It tastes like sweets.
It smells like a rose.
It looks like a happy face.
It sounds like people singing.
It feels like a flower petal.

Julia Cassin (10)
St Clement's RC Primary School, Runcorn

INSIDE THE BOX

Inside the box you will find a maroon mouse dancing.
Inside the box you will find a turquoise cat jumping.
Inside the box you will find a scarlet fruitbat clapping.
Inside the box you will find a blue worm singing.
Inside the box you will find a red baby squirrel swinging.
Inside the box you will find a black fox climbing.
Inside the box you will find a brown badger reading.
Inside the box, inside the box.

Inside the box you will find a purple owl line dancing.
Inside the box you will find a silver duck falling.
Inside the box you will find a green woodmouse acting.
Inside the box you will find pink woodlice playing.
Inside the box you will find a white beetle crawling.
Inside the box you will find a yellow hedgehog running.
Inside the box you will find a gold tiger painting.
Inside the box, inside the box.

Kirsty Hill (9)
St Clement's RC Primary School, Runcorn

MY RABBIT FLOPPY

My rabbit floppy just looks like a poppy.
Although he is not red he has a cute little head.
He bounces in his cage and looks like he's on the stage.
All he needs now is a microphone and maybe a dog's bone.
Now it's time to go to bed.
Floppy please get off my head.
Now it's morning, go and get back in your cage.
I will get you a crowd and do your show proud.

Jenny Bailey (10)
St Clement's RC Primary School, Runcorn

INSIDE THE BOX

Inside the box you will find . . .

An orange spider jumping,
a green centipede running,
an indigo butterfly doing the splits,
a blue woodlouse snoring,
a pink ladybird sewing,
a yellow ant absailing,
a brown bluebottle buzzing,
and a tiny silver worm fast asleep.

Inside the box you will find . . .

A gold moth skipping,
a red and blue bee dancing,
a maroon beetle singing,
a lilac daddy longlegs banging the drums,
a white wasp playing the xylophone,
an emerald cricket playing its tune,
and all together they're a multicoloured band!

Michelle Jones (10)
St Clement's RC Primary School, Runcorn

SPRING!

Spring helps the flowers grow.
It helps the animals stay alive by gobbling up the grass like turkeys.
It makes me so cheerful when a new animal is born.
The cuteness of a chick makes me so happy.
Now plant some more flowers to make a garden colourful.

Thomas Capewell (8)
St Clement's RC Primary School, Runcorn

SPRING!

Spring is a happy day because the birds
Are singing on the garden shed,
Like a soft teddy to cuddle in bed.

All baby animals are being born,
Little chicks are singing songs.
All the flowers waving in the sun,
The sun smiles too much!

Baby lambs running with cheer,
Spring is a happy time of year!
I love spring because flowers are
Waving in the gleaming sun.
Beautiful chicks to cuddle at the farm.
They seem to smile at me all the time.

Rachel Stewart (7)
St Clement's RC Primary School, Runcorn

A LOT OF GOOD DAYS

In the morning I get out of bed
I see glowing light through the curtains.
I look out of my window and I see the lovely colours of the sun,
Yellow, orange and red spreading all over the blue sky.
Then when I go to bed I see the sun setting.
The glowing grey moon and the silver stars shining at my house.
It is just waiting to go down for another beautiful day
To start all over again.
So the sun will come out to brighten up my day,
So beautiful I might go out to play all day and every day
Then I can't wait till another day,
So I can't wait till the days are ours again.

Dominic Jones (9)
St Clement's RC Primary School, Runcorn

SPRING!

Spring is a happy time of year.
Spring is a cheerful time of year.
Spring is a merry time of year.
Spring is a jolly time of year.
You are happy, cheerful, merry and jolly
because the plants are growing and not dying,
I think!

Spring is a time of year
to go in the garden,
to do gardening.
It makes me overjoyed to see the sun
for the first time this year.

Spring is sunny,
(like the yolk out of a fried egg!)
To go in the garden and play,
and to do some sunbathing.
After that,
you are hungry (like a wolf)
happy, (like a wolf who's just eaten)
cheerful, (like a mother wolf who's had a baby wolf)
merry and jolly (like a postman on a sunny morning).

Grace Dargan (8)
St Clement's RC Primary School, Runcorn

SPRING!

In the trees birds sing like seagulls.
In the farm chicks and lambs run round like mad.
Outside it snows and rains and bulbs like daffodils
And tulips grow all yellow and round and red like the sun.
Have you guessed which season it is? It's spring!

Lee Bishop (8)
St Clement's RC Primary School, Runcorn

HALLOWE'EN

Hooray, it's Hallowe'en, time for a party.
We'll have cakes made with blood
and pies covered with mud.
We can have spaghetti worms
and I'll assure you you'll have the squirms.
We'll cut up some pumpkins
and have a pie,
dare to eat it and you'll die.
We'll have a cup of blood
that tastes very good.
And now I think it's time for bed,
but just before I get in
I think I'll try a bit of gin,
Mum get the bin.

Danielle Cosgrove (10)
St Clement's RC Primary School, Runcorn

OPPOSITES

Elephants are big, ants are small.
Coal is black, snow is white.
Manchester I love, Liverpool I hate.
Apples are healthy, chocolate is fattening.
Spaghetti Bolognese is yuk and sweets are yummy!
Teachers are mean and children are kind.
Limousines are long and Minis are short.
Barnsley's shirt is red and Everton's shirt is blue.
I am rich and my sister is poor.
One glass was full and one was empty.
One coat was real fur and one was fake.
The boy had a dog and the girl had a cat.
This poem is by Liam or is it by Truscott.

Liam Truscott (10)
St Clement's RC Primary School, Runcorn

BAD LUCK

Work is horrible,
disgusting and mean,
I sneezed on it
then it was green!

That was bad luck
for me of course,
I turned around,
in came a horse!

I got scared
for it came straight at me,
a horse's hoof
is all I could see.

Two black eyes,
one bloody nose,
a busted lip,
and ten broken toes.

I went to the hospital,
in the horse came,
he came to apologise,
I said the same.

James Capewell (10)
St Clement's RC Primary School, Runcorn

ORANGE STRIPES IN THE GRASS

Orange stripes in the grass,
there lays a tiger ready to prance.
Keeping low,
the river does flow.
Stalking his prey,
he leaps onto a bird of grey.
What goes on in the tiger's mind
nobody will ever find.
You can hear the heavy paws pound,
while the tiger walks along the ground.
The sun's hot beam
makes the tiger want a drink from the stream.
Snap!
He hears a twig crack!
Turning around
without making a sound.
There slithers a snake,
that's no mistake.
A snarl escapes from the tiger's mouth,
then a bite comes from the south.
There is no longer orange stripes in the grass.

Rachael Dunbar (10)
St Clement's RC Primary School, Runcorn

THE FOREST

The forest is beautiful,
especially the leaves on the trees.
They're shiny and they remind me of frogs.
The sea is like the sky,
The sand is so yellow like a star shining in the sky.

Jamie Bennett (8)
St Clement's RC Primary School, Runcorn

SPRING

Spring is like a gold ring.
Spring is like a bell that goes ding, ding, ding.
Spring is like a wing on a bird.
Spring is like a popstar singing on a stage.
Spring is like a ping pong ball flying in the sky.
Spring is like everything.

Danny O'Donnell (10)
St Clement's RC Primary School, Runcorn

SUNSETS

As the shining sun goes down, down, down,
The blue sky turns orange, red, orange, red,
The grass turns dark green, light green, dark green, light green,
All the white clouds turn grey, the little bits of blue sky disappears,
Out comes the thick black sky.
Then everything goes black, nobody can see.

Kayley Taylor (8)
St Clement's RC Primary School, Runcorn

NIGHT TO DAY

The wind is whooshing, the sky is grey,
the trees are blowing,
leaves fall away.
I'm up,
I'm restless,
I can't go to sleep,
it's raining, it's pouring,
all my family are snoring,
this is very, very boring.
I can't believe it, I'm on my own
and I'm watching the Ozone,
it must be day because the
rain and wind have gone away.
Now the sun has come
let's go out and . . .
run,
       run,
            run.

Jemma Carswell (9)
St Clement's RC Primary School, Runcorn

THE LOVELY FOREST

The summer is here,
and the sun is hot.
The trees in the forest are growing.
The forest is big and lovely,
you can see the hot sun
and trees grow up to the sky.

Brittany Moores (9)
St Clement's RC Primary School, Runcorn

WATER

Water, water,
Like the way you cut a cake in quarters.
Little fish run up and down.
The sea looks up at the sky
But things in water can kill good things.
The water is a world.
The sea goes to England and Spain.
Water is life for the people,
But the sea can kill people.
At times the sea is good for fish.
The sky is like a mum and dad.
I love the water.

Michael Richardson (10)
St Clement's RC Primary School, Runcorn

WHERE THE FOREST MEETS THE SEA

I went to a forest but I had to cross the sea.
The sea was blue and clear.
I reach the beach. There was lots of rocks staring at me.
When I went in the forest I saw lots of trees.
Someone said 'There used to be dinosaurs with big sharp claws,
they were not very kind.'
Then I went deep in the forest where I found a hut.
I pretended there were children playing just like me.
When I came back I thought what it will be like soon.

David Farnan (8)
St Clement's RC Primary School, Runcorn

TIGER

Using his wits, his eyes on the prey,
making sure it does not go away.
Of his wits he uses every last ounce,
the tiger is getting ready to *pounce!*
A small growl, it pricks up its ears,
looking around to see what it hears.
The prey's back is turned, the tiger has advanced,
on the deer on which it had glanced.
The deer sees the tiger and runs away,
the deer is gone but the tiger it stays.
For the tiger has to look after its young,
then suddenly hears a flock of bird song.
He sees the birds on the branch above,
his eyes closely on the meal he will love.
Using his wits, his eyes on the prey,
making sure it does not go away.

Benjamin Reynolds (9)
St Clement's RC Primary School, Runcorn

PARADISE ISLAND

Up, down, across and round.
Blue, green, tropical fish.
Slithery snakes, sugary sand.

The fish are jumping up and down,
Round and round we look at the greenery.
The hot golden sun with the clear blue sky,
It's paradise all around.

Elizabeth Farnworth (8)
St Clement's RC Primary School, Runcorn

PETS

Pets, pets, what can you do with pets?
Dogs barking everywhere you go.
Pets, pets, snakes crawling on every road.
Pets, pets, mice running down the street.
Pets, pets, cats saying miaow, miaow.
Pets, pets, rabbits hopping all around.
Pets, pets, lizards hopping on people.
Pets, pets, birds flying about.
Pets, pets, fish swimming through the water.
Pets, pets, they're everywhere you go.

Charlotte Russell (9)
St Clement's RC Primary School, Runcorn

THE FOREST AND SEA

The sea is blue,
The forest is green,
They're very nice colours,
They all go together,
Like the sky meets the sea.
I like both colours,
They're very pretty too.
Like green and blue they remind
Me of the sea and forest.

Heather Birmingham (9)
St Clement's RC Primary School, Runcorn

THE WORLD WOULD BE A BETTER PLACE IF . . .

Nobody threw litter on the floor,
Nobody played knock and run on the old lady's door,
Nobody hurt each other,
Nobody picked on my brother,
Nobody started a fight,
Nobody kidnapped children at night,
Nobody started a war,
Nobody wrote on other people's doors,
Nobody called other people names,
Nobody played fighting games,
Nobody called other people's belongings,
Nobody broke other people's things.

Lauren Garaven (9)
St Clement's RC Primary School, Runcorn

EVEN THOUGH I DO NOT SHOW IT

Mum, Dad and Louis too,
Even though I don't show it, I love you.
I don't mean it when I'm naughty,
But it isn't fair! You're always blaming me Mum.
That's why it is not fair.
I love you all with all my heart.
I'm sorry.

Claire Stubbs (9)
St Clement's RC Primary School, Runcorn

Rats And Mice

I was playing football against the wall,
until I lost my ball.
I went around to the man's house,
and heard a squeaking mouse.
I went and complained to the man,
that mice were under his van.
I knocked again so he went to my mother,
she wasn't in so he went to my brother.
There was a bit of an argument
then after that, they got bit by a rat.
The man ended up with seven toes
and half a nose.
When my mum came in she was very upset,
after all that had happened what would you expect!

Stephen Ellams (10)
St Clement's RC Primary School, Runcorn

The Sand And The Sea

The snake slithers across the golden sand.
The boat is sailing across the clear blue sea.
The colourful fish are slithering in the sea.
The boy is swimming and so are we.
The tropical fish go round and round,
They jump up and down.

Antonia Cook (9)
St Clement's RC Primary School, Runcorn

THIS AND THAT

Crocodile's teeth are like a dungeon of nails.
Black skies in the evening, black as nights.
Winds whooshing, windows swooshing.
My puppy is so cute he likes to play the flute.
I dream about going up there in the air.
The stars in the evening oh so bright.
The rain is pouring down out there, what will I do?
I have to go somewhere.
I read a book last week about dungeons, spiders, crocodiles too.
All we walk on is a blue and green carpet around a ball of rock.
Waterfalls glisten like glitter sparkling on a summer's day.
Dragons' fire is oh so hot and red.

Rebecca Brown (10)
St Clement's RC Primary School, Runcorn

BIRDS

If I were a bird
I would fly across the world
To France, Spain, Hollywood too.
I would sit up in the treetops,
Watching everyone and everything.
When it comes to dark
I would sit in my nest staring at the moon.

Francesca Blake (9)
St Clement's RC Primary School, Runcorn

TEACHERS

Teachers are mean,
Teachers are cruel,
But they still make us come to school.
They shout,
They nag,
They take our school bags!
They eat our dinner,
To make us thinner.
So that is my teacher,
Sometimes is a preacher,
And tells us all what to do!
That is my teacher, Mr Barrow

Melissa Kavanagh (9)
St Clement's RC Primary School, Runcorn

FULL UP

Easter is nearing,
The eggs are on the shelf.
If you don't buy one,
I'll eat them all myself.

Then I will become just like an egg,
Round and squishy,
But not in the head.

Nealey Swadkins (9)
St Clement's RC Primary School, Runcorn

MY DOG

My dog is faster than a train,
He zooms past an aeroplane,
He swims in the deep blue sea
And comes straight home to me.
We cuddle up by the fire,
We sit there for over an hour.
Then we watch some TV,
Nick is on 'Whoopee!'
My mum said, 'It's time for bed.'
I say 'Goodnight' and kiss his head.
He lies alone in his bed.

Leanne May (9)
St Clement's RC Primary School, Runcorn

SCHOOL

School is good,
School is great,
School is full of love,
School is fun,
I like school because
I like getting homework,
School is full of work.

Jade Mayers (9)
St Clement's RC Primary School, Runcorn

THE UNDERGROUND VILLAGE

There is a strange noise
Underground
I don't know what it is!
It sounds like strange people
Talking!
Or a steam train
Going 'Fizz, fizz, fizz!'
Now I can see the ground
Moving up and down
Near where the noise is
At last it has stopped
It has left behind a funny thing
Dark and round
I have found out what it is
Of course, it's a hole
Leading to an underground village!

Nicola Peel (9)
St John's CE Primary School, Sandbach

FROST

Frost has covered the land
In the night.
I am in my back garden
The ground is pure white.
The spiders' webs are
Shining like silver.
I feel very, very cold.
I can feel a small breeze
I shiver and I shake and I freeze.
I feel upset now it's gone.

Joseph Clarke (9)
St John's CE Primary School, Sandbach

SUNNY DAYS

It is a very sunny day
I'm going out to play.
All the birds are chirping
Along the sunny way.
It's peaceful all around,
And I am on the beach.
I go in the sea
I fall and cut my knee.
Now it's time for our picnic,
Mum's had her cake.
I have my sandwiches on a
Big red plate.
After that I go back
Into the sea.
Some boys and girls
Start to bully me.
I run away as fast as I can
I nearly run into the ice-cream van.

Katie Bowler (9)
St John's CE Primary School, Sandbach

AT THE SEASIDE

Get out the T-shirts,
Get out the hats,
And get out the shorts.
Find your sandals,
Find your nets,
Pick up your kites,
And pick up your nets.
Jump in the car,
Fasten your belts.

Jilly Wright (9)
St John's CE Primary School, Sandbach

FROST

Frost has covered the land
In the night
I am in my backyard.
The ground is so hard
And covered with frost
The trees are curling
Over me.
The bushes are coming
Nearer and nearer.
I feel so scared that I tremble
I can hear the whirling
Of the wind and the
Whooshing of waves.
I try to get away, but a feeling
Won't let me leave
This amazing sight.
I walk in slowly.
I feel better now that
I am away from the frost.

Emily Howard (8)
St John's CE Primary School, Sandbach

THE HAIRY SPIDER

I can see a spider,
It's in the sink.
I scream as loud as I can.
It has hairy legs
And a huge body.
Its eyes are big and red.

Kayleigh Ellis (9)
St John's CE Primary School, Sandbach

WINDY DAYS

It is a very windy day!
I am in my bedroom.
Trees are blowing down
I can see litter
Floating about.
I can see people's hats
Blowing off!
I feel scared
I go outside
I let people into my house.
I feel better now
So do the people!

Steven Buckley (9)
St John's CE Primary School, Sandbach

WATER

Water can float on the surface.
I can hear the waves whooshing
Against the rocks and walls.
The sea water is really salty,
If I swallow it
It tastes horrible!
If we did not have water
We would not live.
I like water!

Rebecca Bratt (9)
St John's CE Primary School, Sandbach

WINDY DAYS

It is a very windy day!
I am at home in my garden.
I can see leaves
Blowing across the grass.
The trees are swaying
From side to side.
I can hear dustbins falling.
I feel cold and scared.
I go inside
I put the fire on
I feel happy now.

Sharon Kunz (8)
St John's CE Primary School, Sandbach

A WINDY DAY

It is a very windy day!
I am in the garden.
I can see the trees swaying
I can see hats blowing off!
I can hear the wind whistling
I feel cold and scared
I go in my house
I sit by the fire
I feel warm.

Philip Greenwood (8)
St John's CE Primary School, Sandbach

WINDY DAYS

It is a very windy day!
I am in my garden
I can see leaves blowing about
I can see the trees swaying
The litter is flying around.
I can hear trees rustling.
I can hear the wind whistling.
I feel very cold
I bend over into the wind.
Now I feel better.

Matthew Fithon (8)
St John's CE Primary School, Sandbach

MY PET SPIDER

I can see my pet spider
It is in the bath
I like my pet spider
It's got a very small head
Its eyes are looking at me
It's got a big hairy body
It's got thin hairy legs
It's scuttling in the bath
I can't catch it
It looks like a big black blob.

Yuk!

Eleanor White (9)
St John's CE Primary School, Sandbach

WINDY DAYS

It is a very windy day!
I am at the park
I can see litter
Rolling around
I can see trees bending
I can see the swings
Swinging to and fro.
I can hear the wind whistling
I can hear leaves rustling
I feel scared
I feel cold
I go inside
With my mum
I feel much better now!

Keelie Grindley (9)
St John's CE Primary School, Sandbach

ANIMALS OF THE WORLD

Pigs are fat and pink
Cows are black and white
Hens are red and orange
And sheep are just white!
Cats are brown and black
Dogs are ginger and white
And a horse is just white!

Ruth Mellor (9)
St John's CE Primary School, Sandbach

FROST

Frost has covered the land
In the night.
I am in the garden.
The ground is white.
The cars have ice on them.
The frost makes me cold.
I can hear the wind blowing.
I go in and put my hat on
And my gloves.
I feel better now.

Jodie Ross-Jones (9)
St John's CE Primary School, Sandbach

COLOUR

The grass so green, a flower so red,
a gate so blue and a sun a brilliant gold.

The house so brown, the roof so red
a new bike shining a lovely pink.

A daffodil yellow like the yellow
buttercups dancing in the sun.
The wind blowing in my face tells
me the sign of spring.

Helen Gracie (9)
St John's CE Primary School, Sandbach

FROST

Frost has covered the land
In the night.
I am outside
At home.
The ground is hard, white, cold.
It is damp and freezing.
The frost is white.
I can hear owls making noises.
I am playing outside
It is cold.
I go inside my home.

Arnold Smith (9)
St John's CE Primary School, Sandbach

FISH

Fish are peaceful, gentle and silent
Fish are calm
You can watch them day after day, night after night
Their tails swishing side to side
Everywhere quiet inside
Too peaceful for me.

Elanor Henry (8)
St John's CE Primary School, Sandbach

THE MOON

The moon is like some dirty chalk.
Dusty, rocky and white.
The bright glow in the sky,
Is such a mysterious sight.

The moon is always very bright,
Miles and miles away,
The moon is next to the earth,
It comes up every day.

The moon spins all around the world,
Every day and night,
It always spins around the world,
Always big and bright.

The moon is all around the stars.
Sometimes lonely and glum,
It comes out on the darkest night,
Miles away from the sun.

The moon is way up in the sky,
In the sky all the time,
The moon is smaller than the earth,
I hope you like this moon rhyme.

Rachel Gallagher (11)
St Vincent's Junior School, Altrincham

MOON

The jolly old Mister Moon,
His surface is filled with darkness and gloom.
Think how lonely it must have been
'Til Neil Armstrong came down in Apollo 11
Our old moon looking down on the Earth
Sometimes it must cause silent mirth
The moon is our neighbour, our friend, our bro'
You've got to like it, it'll be there tomorrow.
The moon's fine surface, dusty and grey
It must be a billion years old but what the hey!
The moon's craters, many miles deep,
It must be thousands and thousands of downward feet
The moon is not a planet, not a star,
It is quite close to us, but then, quite far.

The moon is our satellite, orbiting the Earth
It was there even before the first man's birth.

Christopher Ashton (10)
St Vincent's Junior School, Altrincham

PLANTS

A plant ain't such a wonderful thing,
The pollen makes your nose go *ting!*
Nectar's nasty stuff,
And the smell is really duff.
Take the Venus flytrap for example
Flies think it's really rough
It holds on tight, just like a handcuff.

Martin Redhead (10)
St Vincent's Junior School, Altrincham

THE MOON

I'm feeling tired and ready for bed,
Before I lay down my sleepy head,
Just a quick glance through the window,
I see the moon.
It's such a delight to see him at night,
He shines with glory like a shining knight in armour.

The sky lights up, gleaming, beaming with energy,
It will soon be morning,
As the moon starts yawning
His time is up,
He is ready for bed,
Sleepyhead,
Until another night.

Goodnight!

Sarah Keegan (11)
St Vincent's Junior School, Altrincham

MY NOISY BODY

My heartbeat sounds like a beating drum,
And I do a little gulp when I'm afraid
But the part of my body I use most is my mouth.
My mouth does any sound I want it to,
It's great when you're in trouble,
It puts a little word in now and again,
But sometimes it can be a pain.

Theresa Flynn (9)
St Vincent's Junior School, Altrincham

THE MOON

Last night, last night, I looked at the white moon,
My name is Neil Armstrong. I'll go up there soon,
Up in a rocket, the 'Apollo' missions I'll start.
Boy is it fast, it flies like a dart!

Last night, last night, I flew up to the moon,
The journey took three days, it started at noon.
It was kinda' fun being weightless in space,
The best part was landing on the moon, it was ace.

Last night, last night, down the ladder I went,
As my foot touched the moon, it felt weird and bent.
I did a huge jump, cleared about ten-foot,
I love this place, it's a joke, it's a hoot!

Last night, last night, back to Earth I sped,
The module was burning up, I could be dead!
Earth came into sight, the ocean as well,
The parachutes opened, back to Earth, slowly, we fell.

John Charles Peden (10)
St Vincent's Junior School, Altrincham

MY NOISY BODY

My heart beats, it beats faster when I run.
My throat gulps when I swallow.
My ears go pop when I go up high
When they are locked I can only just hear.

Dominic Flynn (9)
St Vincent's Junior School, Altrincham

A MOON POEM

As I looked at the dark old moon,
I thought how lonely it must be,
It looks like lumpy rice pudding,
Without a single tree.

As I looked at the scary old moon,
I thought how different it must be,
Compared with lovely green Earth,
With no air for me.

I looked at the beautiful Earth,
I put it behind my thumb,
It's quite funny actually,
Because I can't hear myself hum.

Josh O'Brien (11)
St Vincent's Junior School, Altrincham

MY NOISY BODY

My body is noisy,
Like a train it is,
The heart pounding, like a funnel,
Lungs inhaling, like the wheels,
After running, like the train stop
at the station, pounding heavily
for a drink of water.

Jonathan Loughrey (9)
St Vincent's Junior School, Altrincham

Moon Poem

The moon is a sloppy
silver-coloured meat pie
It is there,
slumped in the super starry sky.

Neil Armstrong proved,
that the moon isn't made of cheese.
It is made of greyish sand,
that doesn't have a breeze.

The moon is like a sultana,
in the starry sky.
When the morning comes,
the moon says 'Goodbye.'

Carl Hynes (11)
St Vincent's Junior School, Altrincham

Cactus!

C acti have lots of spikes
A nd this is the plant that
    everybody likes!
C acti are cool.
T hat is the rule
U nlike some other plants that are dull.
S o that's why cacti are really
                        Cool!

Francesca Wellock (10)
St Vincent's Junior School, Altrincham

OLD PEOPLE

Old people
Got more experience
Never know what they're going to do or say
'Life is precious' that's what they say,
'Don't waste it.'
Grandmas and grandads
So much fun to have
So much fun to share
Telling you about their life
When they were as young as me
Wrinkles, glasses, that's what they have
Reading the newspaper
Knitting cardigans and jumpers
Wishing they were young again
While we wish we were older.
So happy to hear what I did today
So interested to hear what I have to say
They can get annoying because
They know more than me,
But it's very interesting that they're there
When I need help.
Old people
Grandmas and grandads I love them
What would I do without them?

Emily Pope (10)
St Vincent's Junior School, Altrincham

MY NOISY BODY

My body makes a lot of noise
It seems to happen just to boys
My heart goes *bang!*
My ears go *pop!*
My throat crackles after I've sung.

Dominic Preugschat (9)
St Vincent's Junior School, Altrincham

ALIEN IN THE CUPBOARD

I was sitting in my bed,
When I heard a funny noise,
Coming from the cupboard full of toys.
I walked to the cupboard,
And opened up the door,
An alien popped out.
It was big and green,
But it didn't look mean.
I asked it its name,
And it said it was 'Shane',
It closed the doors,
Set off to space,
Smoke pouring into my room,
There it goes . . .
Zooooooooom!

Dean Webster (8)
Underwood West Junior School

ALIENS

Green aliens coming to Earth
Running people everywhere
Everyone shouting
Everyone running
No one stops

A world empty
Lives gone forever
It's empty forever
Echoes I hear but what?
Nearly everyone had disappeared
Someone there but who?

Jennifer Davies (9)
Underwood West Junior School

EIGHTY ALIENS

Surrounding me,
Aliens stink,
Based in space,
I don't think.
Aliens blue,
Aliens green.
Some are smelly,
Some are clean.
UFO, flying high in the sky.

Zachary Baker (9)
Underwood West Junior School

SPACE

Stars in the sky,
Planets turning around in space,
Asteroids floating around,
Comets blazing fire,
Earth travelling around the sun.

Stacey Palin (8)
Underwood West Junior School

SPACE

S tars in the sky
P lanets high above
A steroids flying past
C omets whizzing everywhere
E arth travelling around.

Mark Welsh (9)
Underwood West Junior School

SPACE RIDE

Rockets blazing all day long,
Clanking.
Red, pink and green,
Sparkling stars through the night,
Rushing through the sky.

Katy Western 8)
Underwood West Junior School

FIRE

Fire squirting
everywhere,
I was very, very scared,
Racing to get out of the
door away from the
flames,
Everyone running
around in rings,
Someone died, clouds
of smoke everywhere.

Alexandra Scarlett (8)
Underwood West Junior School

CRUNCHING, MUNCHING

Crunching, munching,
Man on the moon.
Here we come very soon.
Into space in a rocket
Up into the jet-black sky.

Carly Metcalfe (8)
Underwood West Junior School

LIFT-OFF

Up goes the rocket raining fire,
Exploding flames up in the sky.
Stars shooting, all fiery hot,
Melting, munching up the sunlit sky,
Crunching clouds all over the Earth,
As the rocket sets off.

Michaela Readdin (9)
Underwood West Junior School

MOON

Moon yellow and bumpy
Ice on Pluto and
Neptune.
Looking at shooting
stars.
Kicking sparks
everywhere.
Yellow stars.
Whooshing comets
sparkling around space.
Aliens all green and
slimy feet with five eyes.
Yellow moon like sand.

Matthew Birtwistle (8)
Underwood West Junior School

SPACE

Racing off into space,
Off to Venus or Mars.
Carrying an important probe.
Kilometres of rock and dust.
Eager to find an alien.
Tall green monsters *'Arrgh!'*
Back inside on our way home.

Ricky Gray (8)
Underwood West Junior School

GREEN ALIENS

Gloomy green aliens came down from space.
Racing around my garden, grass getting slimy.
Everlasting on our Earth.
Entering my bedroom, scared stiff.
Nearby, another green alien appeared, moving
menacingly.
A silvery spaceship spinning,
round and round,
leaving a bright light on my grass.
I saw another person inside the spaceship.
Everywhere, including the sun was changing
colours,
like a blue-green colour.
Nearly everyone hypnotised, unable to move.
Space stars flaring and falling,
destroying the Earth.

Rachel Johnson (9)
Underwood West Junior School

SPACE

Soaring up into the sky,
Prepared for anything,
Amazing brilliant view
Stretching ahead,
Coming from the ship,
Extraordinary images
Coming down from
Mars.

Samantha Florence Lee (9)
Underwood West Junior School

ALIENS

A spaceship landed in
my garden,
Looking straight at us
were some aliens.
Icy feet walking on the
grass.
Every footstep walking
towards us.
Nearer and nearer then
turning around he went
back to his spaceship.
Spaceship flying in the
sapphire sky.

Rachel Louise Leech (9)
Underwood West Junior School

ALIEN

There was once an alien from Mars.
Who just loved to make his own cars.
He painted them all green
So that they couldn't be seen
By the bad aliens called Travines.
The king Travine had nine toes,
And one really big nose.
His hands were really
            gigantic and fantastic.

Christopher Tomkinson (8)
Underwood West Junior School

MARS

Moon floating in the
air.
Aliens running
everywhere.
Rockets floating in
space.
Aliens floating in
space and everywhere.

Steven Mostyn-Harratt (8)
Underwood West Junior School

MY SISTER

My sister acts like an alien,
Dreaming about laser guns
and astronauts.
She will never leave me alone.
She scared me with her alien mask,
It's like watching a horror film.
Always imagining that
there's a spaceship outside.

Charlton Reid (8)
Underwood West Junior School

THINGS IN SPACE

Whizzing space shuttles around space.
Checking out moons and planets
UFOs I can imagine
Might be visiting our planets.
I see stars bright and sparkly
And a moon I see as well.
You never know what's out there,
From aliens to UFOs.

Andrzej Pogonowski (8)
Underwood West Junior School

ASTRONAUTS

Astronauts are floating around.
Everywhere in different directions.
Searching for hidden planets
Are there aliens?
Ask one who knows,
said Jack.

Jaçk Taylor (9)
Underwood West Junior School

TORNADO

I stood alone on the hill,
With the roar of the night storm around.
The rain shot down,
Like bullets from a gun.
The wind,
A tiger of eternal life.
The dense mist spreads over the hillside,
Like water from a jug.
It's life,
As long as time itself.
Still the wind prowls around me,
Blowing my hair like a hairdryer.
A vortex forms around my body,
A whirlpool of air.
I'm sucked two feet off the ground,
I rise higher,
The wind is heavy now,
I'm floating effortlessly,
Higher and higher.
The tornado has begun.

Matthew Hallsworth (10)
Victoria Road CP School

THE STORM

A deafening silence filled the air
As the storm clouds roll silently over.
Then a sudden crash as raging winds stampeded
Through the air with a mighty rip.
Violent lightning struck, then silence
                        as the clouds roll on.

Joseph Santley (11)
Victoria Road CP School

THE STORM

Calm before the storm
Quiet before the wind
Mild and still before the rain
Clouds as black as coal.

The mighty wind like a tornado
Swirling around forever
Howling as loud as a werewolf
Darkness is all around.

Booming thunder
Flashing lights
Terrified children
Lightning as bright as the sun.

Raging downpours
In the greatest storm
One last boom!
Then at last it ends!

Stephanie Draper (11)
Victoria Road CP School

THE LAST DAY OF THE FIRST WORLD WAR

We were terrified after a flare blew up.
Zoom, it went.
Hear the Captain shout 'Charge!'
With fright I jumped out with my gun
Then, *Bang!*
Then into the dark night freezing cold.
I am lying there in the freezing cold, injured.
I am thinking, will I die
Or will I get home?

Thomas Jeffs (8)
Victoria Road CP School

THE MONSTER STORM

The clouds blacken, black as coal,
The wind cries like a lost soul,
The thunder booms like an angry lord,
The lightning strikes like a murdering sword,
The rain pours like a drowning cascade,
A monster storm has now been made!

This monster rampages all through the night,
Until it fades off and goes out of sight,
The monster stops with one mighty boom,
And a bolt of lightning to light up the room,
Then it leaves Runcorn to sleep in peace,
Or, until the morning comes at least.

Stephanie Connell (10)
Victoria Road CP School

THE BATTLE WITH THE GERMANS

As the fight begins we walk across the no-man's land,
To fight the Germans at the other side waiting for us.
The German Captain fires at us, he fires bullets and gas.
We quickly put our gas masks on and quickly run away.

Boom! Boom! Boom! go the bullets coming from the guns,
As we hear our Captain shout 'Charge!'
We run towards each other but keep on falling over.

Nearly everyone is dead and lying in their graves.

Kelly Jones & Siobhan Sifflett (8)
Victoria Road CP School

THE ANGRY STORM

One cold night,
The sky was as black as coal
Overhead were clouds,
They were like piles of rubbish in bin bags.
The rain started,
It was like guns' bullets.
The clouds got darker,
Like angry elephants.
The rain got heavier,
Like stones falling from a cliff.
It got windy.
It howled through doorways,
Like a hooting owl.
The thunder came,
It was like a roaring lion.
The lightning shot down like a shooting star,
Flashing like a sword.
It died down,
Like a composer stopping an orchestra.

Sian Lloyd (10)
Victoria Road CP School

THE STORM

The deafening silence drifts
Around the town
Rumbling clouds ride across
The black sky
Lightning strikes like a yellow flash
Downpours of rain
And then just silence.

Paul Knowles (11)
Victoria Road CP School

THE FIRST WORLD WAR

All the soil is turning into squelching mud
Do you feel freezing cold
And can you feel the dripping water
Making all your body cold?

Can you hear the captain call 'Charge.'
The men are gasping for breath.
'All the best,'
Says the cheering crowd.

Can you hear the explosions?
Bang! Bang!
'Quick, we need our gas masks'
Say all the men.

Dark flashes of light
Help! I've been shot
Rats' footprints everywhere
I would not dare to go anywhere
Will we ever get home?

Nicola Monteith & Nicola Spencer (8)
Victoria Road CP School

STORM

Inky black clouds bring,
Darkness over the town,
As silent as the dead.
Winds blow violently,
Rain falls, lightning flashes,
As bright as the sun.
Animals hiding in their nests.

Paul Magee (11)
Victoria Road CP School

THE FIRST WORLD WAR

Flashes of light in the dark air, only of a flare.
Squish squelch is all I hear, dripping raindrops
are overhead.
'Charge,' shouts our leader firing with his gun
Boom! Boom! Boom!
Rats scurrying through the mud,
And men reaching for their gas masks.

And then . . .
Silence!

Chloe Reilly (8)
Victoria Road CP School

THE FIRST WORLD WAR

I am frightened.
I can hear lots of explosions everywhere.
I see people dead
I see people injured.
Some people rolling down hills.
I cannot hear anything except the guns.
Why do they have to do this?
I shoot everywhere.
I want my mum.
I am really, really scared.

Katie Blackburn (7)
Victoria Road CP School

WORLD WAR 1

In the middle of the night
rats are scurrying
and it makes me shiver.

I see the coppery mud
with the footprints of the rats
and their smell is unbearable.

Bang! A gas bomb went off,
masks on, don't breathe it in.
Bang! Bang! Bang! Boom! Boom! Boom!

I hear the thud of guns
I hear the screaming
My watch strikes eleven.

It's the eleventh hour of the eleventh day
Of the eleventh month.
We have silence at last.

Scott Jameson (8)
Victoria Road CP School

THE STORM

The Earth was cold,
The wind whistled,
Rain turned to hail,
The thunder boomed,
The conquering murky clouds,
Sailed away slowly,
And left behind total destruction.

Kyle Burns (11)
Victoria Road CP School

THE AWESOME STORM

It was silent, like night-time,
Skies everywhere had no birds,
Just straightforward stillness.

Intense winds started whirling wildly.
Dark thunderclouds began to appear,
Then echoing thunder commenced.

Dense showers crashed down,
Creating colossal floods,
Crashing through the gloomy city.

Shattering windows everywhere,
Making people afraid,
Another great storm has passed.

Joe Woods (10)
Victoria Road CP School

THE FIRST WORLD WAR

I hear the thud of machine guns
banging near the trenches.
I see the breath coming from the
soldiers' mouths, breathing in their masks.
I hear rats scuttling in the mud.
Sounds of men crying for help.
I hear the sound of flares lighting
up in the dark sky.
I hear the muttering men asking if
they're going to get home
I hear the silence when the war is over.

Derek Wiswall (8)
Victoria Road CP School

THE STORM IN THE VILLAGE

Outside gloomy, calm, still,
All is silent not a sound,
Darkness sneaks across the sky,
Winds howl through the woods,
Trees falling smashing cars,
Thunder gives a fearful roar,
Lightning flashes with a strike,
Rain starts falling.

The rain gets harder,
The thunder gets nearer,
No one can take it anymore,
Faster and faster rain falls,
The storm gets worse,
Oh! Look at that tree,
Down it falls,
Down with a crash!

The storm is settling,
The sun starts shining,
Villagers are happy,
Rainbows start to appear,
No more dark, gloomy clouds,
No more rain falls.

Yvonne Byrom (11)
Victoria Road CP School

THE STORM STRIKES BACK

The world stands still as quiet as a mouse,
Clouds drift across the sky,
As the storm approaches the clouds turn black,
Thunder rumbles,
Lightning strikes,
Children frightened,
In a dark noisy night
The storm is here
How long will it last?
Who knows? Maybe soon
It will pass.
The wind whips up,
The rain lashes down like shower water speeding into the bath,
Clattering dustbins like flying saucers
Getting ready to go back to space,
Branches breaking off the tall, tall trees,
I wonder what damage we can expect to see?
The wind is dying down
The rain has stopped
It's getting quieter
No more banging
No more clanging
I think the storm has stopped.

Mark Hamilton (11)
Victoria Road CP School

THE STORM

Deafening silence, birds flee to
Seek shelter.
Murky black clouds roll across
The sky smothering the sun.
The mighty wind wrecks everything
In sight.
The downpour comes like a jaguar
Pouncing in its prey.
The storm has ended, trees blown down,
Slates blown off,
'Thank goodness it has past over.'

Katie Silcock (10)
Victoria Road CP School

WINTER STORM

On a cold bright winter's day,
Clouds looked heavy and grey.
It started to rain, wind began to blow,
Getting stronger, getting heavier.
Rain changed to hailstones
Wind changed to a gale.
Trees began to sway.
The tiles fell off roofs.
Rubbish swirled down streets.
Nearly got blown off my feet.

Ashia Thompson (10)
Victoria Road CP School

THE STORM'S REVENGE

The quiet afternoon sky turns dark,
The clouds darken rapidly,
As they crawl across the sky,
Like smoke on a battlefield,
Immediately the birds stop singing,
All around is silence, silence.

The silence is shattered,
Like a thousand windows,
As rain starts to beat,
Invincible lightning flashes,
Mighty thunder roars,
Trees and walls tumble,
But heavier, heavier gets the rain.

The water rushes along the road,
Like a raging torrent,
And suddenly it ends,
All is quiet.

David Lawton (11)
Victoria Road CP School

THE STORM

The calm Earth waits anxiously,
Before black clouds roll in,
But the storm has begun,
With thick grey clouds,
As grey as a rock.

The thunder comes followed by,
Lightning, wind and rain,
They turn into hail,
Tapping windows,
Violent winds blow,
Swaying trees,
Slates come off.

Rivers start to overflow,
Flashes of lightning disappear,
The storm has passed now,
But devastation is still here,
But still we're safe,
Safe from danger.

Scott Oliver (10)
Victoria Road CP School

THE STORM

Tempestuous clouds twist over hills and dales,
Enraged with anger,
Boisterous winds arise from nowhere,
With devastating effects.

The wind is howling through keyholes,
Nature at its worst,
Trees uprooted,
Houses damaged,
Will it ever stop?

Deafening silence fills the air as calm returns,
The storm has gone,
The air is quiet,
Earth is at rest again.

Phillip Bartsch (10)
Victoria Road CP School

ON A STORMY NIGHT

In the darkness of the night
There was a rainstorm in sight
Then all of a sudden
There was a shower of rain,
And next came a hurricane.
Trees flying all around, banging,
Shattering, long and loud.
The violent winds roared.
Then moments later there was calm
But destruction left behind.

Kyle Jerram (11)
Victoria Road CP School

THE RAGING STORM

Earth is silent,
No birds singing, no sound at all,
Everywhere motionless,
Grey clouds begin to form.

Magnificent clouds gather,
Making the sky as black as coal,
Torrential rain cascading down.

A rainstorm comes crashing down, wind gushing,
Rattling windows, doors and gates,
Wind is as careless as a bull.

Crash! A bang of thunder,
Flash! A bolt of lightning.
A mighty storm is passing,
A quiet rumble, a flash is all that is left.

Gardens and houses are flooded
Roads blocked with trees
People killed
Seems like everything is dead.

Sarah Holbrook (11)
Victoria Road CP School

STORMY DAYS

The quietness
The peacefulness of everything,
Animals hide in holes
Or bushes,
As if monsters are coming.
Enormous dusky clouds
Were charging
Like animals in a stampede,
A light breeze blows,
Leaves rustle gradually forming
Into a strong wind,
As large branches move
Starts a violent gale!
A gentle rain breaks out
Gradually getting heavier
Till it becomes a torrential downpour.
The lightning suddenly jumped out
Like a firecracker,
Thunder roared
Like a lion!
Then everything slowed down
To a complete stop,
As if nothing had happened,
But the damage was still there.

Andrew Reilly (11)
Victoria Road CP School

THE VIOLENT STORM

The village is peaceful and calm, not a sound
Or sight of anybody or anything, like a tiger
Waiting for its prey.
The village remains in quietness until . . .
The dark clouds cover the still blue sky
The sky turns black and violent winds howl
Across the darkened sky like a wolf howling at a
Full moon.
Bang went the thunder like a drum banging
Crash went the lightning like symbols crashing
The storm ended with an enormous bang.
Trees lay helplessly like a dog with a bad wound.

Sarah Davies (10)
Victoria Road CP School

THE STORM

Earth waits terrified.
Turbulent winds rage.
Inky and black clouds hurtle overhead.
Heavy rain falls like darts.
Violent winds race around like
Bulls in a field.
They rip anything in their way
Silence strikes
The storm is over.

Andrew Jack (10)
Victoria Road CP School

THE RAGING STORM

Silently, violent-looking clouds sweep over
The dark gloomy sky
While the world patiently waits
For the first clash of thunder
And flashes of lightning to strike.

The howling winds burst in
Bringing destruction, windows rattle
Screams, shouts
The storm has begun.

Thunder roars, lightning crashes
The troublesome storm has brought its worst
Destruction, tree after tree falls with a crash
Echoes of the storm shake the troubled earth.

The storm passes, leaves the placid earth to mourn
The sun shines a marvellous coloured smile
The earth is placid once more.

Louise Illidge (11)
Victoria Road CP School

THE STORM

Earth as calm as a baby sleeping,
Stars fading, moon shining.
Then the moon dies. The sky is dismal
Fog covers like a frosty blanket.
The wind blows madly and rain pours.
The thunder rumbles. Lightning crashes
Rivers flood.
The destruction is violent.
Now everything is still and silent.

Kerry Purvis (11)
Victoria Road CP School

STORM

The rain fierce, aggressive,
Plunges down heavily,
To the sorrowful earth.
The flood begins.

Violent destructive winds
Seek out cars like a
Dog after a cat,
They destroy trees like
A chainsaw ripping paper
The *hurricane* begins.

Shadowy overcast skies,
Which overshadow the land
Which is a part of the storm.

The rain stops gently,
Great winds hushed,
Shadowy dull skies blue like a pool.
The storm is over.

Steven Burnett (11)
Victoria Road CP School

A RAGING STORM

The village as silent as a grave
Birds stop singing
Trees desist swaying.
Black clouds rumble over the sky
The storm begins.

Waves crash against the shore
Gates bang and sway in the gusting wind
Windows rattle
Wind howls through the village.

Rain brings floods
Thunder and lightning strikes
Animals hide from the downpouring rain
Cars washed away.

Clouds slowly creep away
Leaving people devastated
It suddenly stops raining
The storm has ended.

Ashley Wright (11)
Victoria Road CP School

THE ANGRY STORM

The calm earth is silent
Clouds are rolling over
The rain drips quietly on the ground.
The wind starts to blow as it howls
Through the trees.
The storm is getting angry.

As the storm gets wilder,
Gates start to bang.
Trees start to swing from side to side.
As the storm gets weaker, everything
Becomes calm.
The calm earth is silent.

John Dutton (11)
Victoria Road CP School

THE DESTRUCTIVE STORM

Animals hide,
The world is silent.
Rumbling clouds tumble blocking the sunlight.
A cloudburst falls to Earth,
As the first thunder crashes,
And lightning strikes.
The storm has begun!
The wind is deathly cold,
Violently it swirls and twirls,
Leaving the damage behind.
Slates crashing, fires howling like wolves,
And trees collapse causing chaos,
The destructive storm has finally finished.
The clouds separate
Light is visible and warmth fills the air.

Faye Schön (11)
Victoria Road CP School

STORMY WEATHER

Still earth, quiet as a lamb.
Nothing moving.
There is silence.
Suddenly rain begins to drizzle.
Gets heavier every minute.
Winds roar powerfully.
Trees crashing down.
Windows crack and smash.
Walls hastily fall.
Everything is destroyed.

Francesca Wright (11)
Victoria Road CP School

THE HORRENDOUS STORM

The dusky sky,
The world as silent as death.
Drizzle falls, winds howl,
Black shadowy clouds,
Cover the dark sky.

The storm has begun,
The violent gales,
The winds as fierce as
The rocking sea.
The blaring lightning
Strikes.
The howling winds,
Tear down the trees.

The storm finally stops,
With the sun and a rainbow
Everything is calm and still.

Kerry-Anne M'Intosh (11)
Victoria Road CP School

THE STORM

The earth is covered with black clouds and
showers of rain.
The wind howls like a wolf howling.
The angry lightning strikes. *Bang!* It's
like a raging fire.
The thunder is uncontrollable like the wind.
The waves are crashing against the rocks.
Trees tumble as the ground vibrates.
The storm has ended and the sun comes out.

Jaclyn Thomas (11)
Victoria Road CP School

THE STORM

Breeze as calm as the sea
Skies greyer than mist
Clouds darker than night
Trees moving like madness.

Thunder roaring like madness
Wind howling like a car
Fences falling every second
Lightning giving me a fright.

You hear a rumble in the distance
The storm has gone away
The breeze is calm once again
A beautiful sound is here.

Mark Crowley (11)
Victoria Road CP School

STORM IS BACK!

Raging clouds rumble,
Casting shadows as black as night.
Violent, windy howls
Screams of horror and fright!
Clashes of lightning strike again,
Thunderous rumbles roar out loud,
But the storm is dying down
Birds fly high,
As the earth gives a gentle sigh
For the *storm* has passed by

Wendy Osborne (11)
Victoria Road CP School

AUTUMN COLOURS

The purple of wine.
The colour of the vine.
It tastes so very sour,
It's full of power.

Automatic orange falls to the ground,
Sizzling citrus lemon and lime.

Rusty brown,
hot lava,
round and round
Bang!
To the ground.

Rebecca Taylor (8)
Willaston CP School

SPRING

Squirrels run
Children have fun
All because of spring.
And the best thing about
it is school's out!

The birds sing a song
and the time goes so long.
So run, run to the
garden of spring.
It is a lovely place
so go there!

Charlotte Wilson (8)
Willaston CP School

SOMETHING FISHY

Happy and graceful watching
the stream.
Feeling like I'm in
a dream.
Nature buzzing all around
me.
While I'm lying under a
willow tree.
Frogs are jumping all
round you.
Rabbits are jumping too.
The waterfalls are
trickling,
And the grass is prickling
all over me.
I feel like dancing
while the deer are prancing
on the forest ground.
A boat slides past as
slow as a snail,
And a small puppy dog
began to wail.
The wail was as loud as
the wind.
That was a poem of my paradise dream.

Samantha Taylor (9)
Willaston CP School

THE RIVER

Clickety-clack, clack, clack
Clickety-click
The steam train chugs past *clickety-clack*
Phoot, phoot. Chug, chug, chug!
'*Tweet, tweet*' the blackbird tweets and sings.
The river flows and the fish swim
Drip, drop, drip drop the rain quietly
patters on the river.
I slowly put my umbrella up and see
the birds go to shelter.
Drip drop it rains harder
I take cover in my tent
Chug, chug, sssh, sssh, sssh along
comes the barge 'The Queen Mary'
it is called
Drip, drop, the rain stops.

Lee Towers (9)
Willaston CP School

HOW I FEEL

I feel like a swan drifting with
relaxation,
I feel like a barge floating out to sea,
I feel like a rabbit running round and
round a tree,
I feel like a bird singing merrily,
I feel like a warm spring day,
I feel as calm as a fish resting,
I feel really sleepy and dreamy.

Kathryn Alcock (9)
Willaston CP School

THE SUNNY SPRING DAY

As peaceful as a spring day when people
go boating night and day
The sun rises on a cloudy day when we go
painting by the lake
Drip, drop, the sun drops and we are over
the hill and far away
The space rabbit is crushing carrots whilst
in the silver moonlight
The floating bird in the air is leaping
everywhere.

Natasha Jackson (9)
Willaston CP School

BY THE RIVER

Flowing happily as a waterfall.
Fishes swimming sweetly on a summer
Spring day.
Rabbits hopping idly round the sharp
Sticking-out grass.
Birds sweetly sing at the romance.
Fish swim calm underwater.
Joyful people sit on the relaxed calm
Smooth grass reading to the swans.
Drift, drift off to sleep.

Aryan Sadler (9)
Willaston CP School

THE RIVER

A calm swan swam swiftly down the river
A small cruiser quietly travelled to the town
The river flows like a cruising car
A cow in the field is mooing softly
A fish is dancing idly in a stream
A man is fishing and he has just caught a salmon
The salmon is jumping in the river
A cricket is playing and playing its tune
A relaxed man is drawing a picture of the river
A woman is sleeping with her children
The ducks are flying happily in the sky
It's getting dark and a boat is driving into the sunset.

Jonathan Colenso (10)
Willaston CP School

SMOOTH AS ICE

As calm as midsummer's wind.
As slow as a snail.
As graceful as a swan.
As beautiful as paradise.
As flowing joyfully as a flying bird.
As idle as a lake.
As relaxed as space.
As'quiet as a soothing wood
As . . .

Jason Perez (10)
Willaston CP School

BY THE RIVER

As smooth as water flowing
As graceful as a swan drifting past
As quiet as rabbits running madly in midsummer air
As peaceful as the calm woods at night
As wondrous as fish swimming past
As slow as a slug
As idle as water
As thoughtful as me drifting past all the planets in space
As sleepy and as calm as nature
As smooth as ice.

Adam Kirkpatrick (10)
Willaston CP School

BY THE RIVER

I was sitting by the river
when a fish came jumping by
it was relaxed, calm, I was dreamy and sad.
Fish went past the waterfall, wondrous it was.
The waterfall was peaceful on this pretty spring day.
There was a tree behind me and a leaf in the river
which was floating as slowly as a snail.

Hannah Wright (9)
Willaston CP School

THE ROMANS

The Romans were a lively lot,
They had a lot of fighters
They fought and fought and died and died
And killed lots of nasty blighters.

The Romans were a nice clean lot,
They had a lot of baths,
They washed and washed and scrubbed and scrubbed
And they had a lot of laughs.

The Romans were an angry lot
They had a lot of fun
They poked and stabbed and sliced and diced
And killed almost everyone!

Nick Powell (10)
Wincham CP School

CHOCOLATE

While walking past the factory
The tempting chocolate heaven,
An overpowering smell was produced
Round about eleven.

A simple bar of gold
With the most luxurious texture,
The magic to behold.
The *fantastic* creamy mixture.

J-J Stannard (11)
Wincham CP School

MY COMPUTER

The small square screen,
The shiny CDs,
The mystery game,
It makes you freeze.
Broken sword, dungeon-keeper,
I think software could be cheaper.

Barp! Barp! Barp!
The printer driver,
Printing a caption about a
Wooden horse and cart.
The computer is mine!
I love it so,
I would be so sad to see it go.

Thomas McGregor (11)
Wincham CP School

THE SNOW

The snow looks like pearls,
It smells like nothing,
It looks a bit like a girl!
It's cold and white,
But it tastes like nothing
            you have ever tasted,
My mum said,
'Go out and play,'
But I hesitated.

Thomas Stringer (10)
Wincham CP School

RABBITS

As I peacefully wandered
Under the bright green trees
With my heavenly rabbit I suddenly . . .
Felt a breeze
A cold and relaxing breeze
My heavenly rabbit was . . . licking me.

My heavenly rabbit kept on tickling me
As we reached the dancing sea
The cold and relaxing sea
I pushed my rabbit away
And then suddenly felt another breeze
My heavenly rabbit was . . . licking me.

David Johnson (10)
Wincham CP School

SNOW

I was walking in the forest
When suddenly I felt a tingle
Falling down on my chest
It was so cold
I knew it could not last
I ran back home and told . . .
The whole cast
About the snow
In the forest
That dribbled down my body to my toe.

Nicole Ashley (10)
Wincham CP School